A S

SWAMI VIVEKANANDA

SWAMI TEJASANANDA

Advaita Ashrama
(Publication Department)
5 DEHI ENTALLY ROAD
CALCUTTA 700 014

Published by
Swami Mumukshananda
President, Advaita Ashrama
Mayavati, Pithoragarh, Himalayas
from its Publication Department, Calcutta

ISBN 81-7505-030-6

Printed in India at
Gipidi Box Co.
3B Chatu Babu Lane
Calcutta 700 014

PUBLISHER'S NOTE
TO THE SECOND EDITION

Since the first appearance of the book certain new findings about the life of Swami Vivekananda have been made. In the present edition the book has therefore been slightly edited and corrected accordingly. We are indebted to Amrita Salm of the Vedanta Society of Southern California for her help in this regard.

10 April 1995   PUBLISHER

PUBLISHER'S NOTE
TO THE SECOND EDITION

Since the first appearance of the book certain new findings about the life of Swami Vivekananda have been made. In the present edition the book has therefore been slightly edited and corrected accordingly. We are indebted to Amrita Sabha of the Vedanta Society of Southern California for their help in this regard.

10 April 1995   PUBLISHER

PREFACE

During his last illness, when Sri Rama-krishna could not talk, he wrote on a piece of paper that Swami Vivekananda (then known as Narendra Nath) should have to work for the good of humanity. But Swami Vivekananda did not relish this idea, since he was yearning to remain absorbed in meditation and enjoy perennial Bliss. Sri Ramakrishna then remarked that if Swami Vivekananda would not willingly plunge into work, the Divine Mother would force him to do it. Afterwards, when Swami Vivek-ananda was in the ceaseless turmoil of work, moving like a meteor from the East to the West, and the West to the East, he used to say, 'Some-thing has possessed me and is giving me no rest.' The period of his active work was short, but posterity will some day be able to assess at its true value all that he has done for his motherland as well as for the world.

Meantime, one is concerned with the fact that the life and message of Swami Vivekananda are a source of great inspiration to many in their individual as well as collective life. His words give courage to a drooping soul, his message brings new hope for a sinking nation. Swami

Vivekananda was the embodiment of strength, and if all his teachings were to be summed up in one word, that word would be STRENGTH—a dynamic strength. It is for the want of strength that individuals fail in life, nations suffer, and the world is in torment. As such, the number of persons who are eager to know about Swami Vivekananda or are likely to be benefited by his message is legion.

The present short biography is intended to meet the needs of those who, with all their earnestness, have neither the time nor the opportunity to read longer works about the Swami. A versatile genius as Swami Vivekananda was, and many-sided as were his activities, it is idle to hope or to expect that a complete picture of that mighty soul could be given in such a small compass. The attempt is here made only to give a glimpse, so that people may become interested to know more about him.

In preparing this book, we have utilized the materials found in the Advaita Ashrama publications about Swami Vivekananda. The present book is a companion volume to *A Short Life of Sri Ramakrishna*.

December 21, 1940
MAYAVATI   PUBLISHER

CONTENTS

CHAPTER   PAGE

I	Boy Narendra Nath	9
II	Meeting With Sri Ramakrishna	22
III	Transformation	34
IV	A Wandering Monk	42
V	From the Old World to the New	56
VI	In the Parliament of Religions	62
VII	As a Teacher in America	70
VIII	In England	77
IX	Beloved India	84
X	Message to his Countrymen	88
XI	In the Company of Western and Eastern Disciples	101
XII	Second Visit to the West	106
XIII	Parting Glimpses	110
XIV	The Passing	117
	Some Utterances	120

In London, 1896

A SHORT LIFE OF SWAMI VIVEKANANDA

I

BOY NARENDRA NATH

The future Swami Vivekananda was born in the famous Datta family of Simla, in Calcutta. His family name was Narendra Nath Datta. His grandfather, Durga Charan Datta, was a gifted man, well versed in Persian and Sanskrit and had a great aptitude for law. But at the age of twenty-five, after the birth of his son, Vishwanath, he renounced worldly life and became a monk. Vishwanath Datta, father of Swami Vivekananda, was also endowed with many qualities of head and heart, for which he commanded great respect from one and all. He was proficient in English and Persian, and took delight in the study of the Bible and the poems of the Persian poet Hafiz. He took to law as a profession and became a successful attorney-at-law in the High Court of Calcutta. He was a man of deep compassion and great sympathy, and his charity very often knew no

discrimination. Vishwanath was a great lover of
music and had a very good voice. He it was
who insisted that his son Narendra Nath should
study music, for he looked upon it as the source
of much pleasure.

Vishwanath was blessed with a wife who
was his peer in all respects. She was
exceptionally intelligent and possessed royal
dignity and fire of one born, as it were, to regal
estate. She won the respect and veneration of all
who came in contact with her, and her
judgement was followed in the conduct of all
affairs that mattered. Calm resignation to the
will of God in all circumstances, strength, and
reserve characterized this Hindu woman. The
poor and the helpless were the special objects of
her solicitude. She was noted for her unusual
memory and knew by heart long passages from
the great epics, the *Ramayana* and the
Mahabharata, which she read daily.

Of such parents was born, on Monday the
12th January 1863, Narendra Nath, who
afterwards as Swami Vivekananda shook the
world, and ushered in a new age of glory and
splendour for India.

The influence of the mother in the
formation of the character and the development
of the mind of a child is always very great.

Narendra Nath used to tell later how his mother had taught him his first English words; and he mastered the Bengali alphabet under her tutorship. It was at her knee that he first heard the tales of the *Ramayana* and the *Mahabharata*. His boyish imagination was captivated by the life of Sri Rama, an incarnation of God, and he purchased a clay image of Sita-Rama and worshipped it with flowers. Sometimes Shiva took the place of Rama as the object of worship by Narendra Nath. But nevertheless the *Ramayana* had the greatest fascination for him; and whenever the *Ramayana* was to be read in the neighbourhood, he was sure to be there. Sometimes he was so enraptured by the thrilling episodes of Rama's life that he forgot all about home. Naren—as he was now called—liked to play at meditation. Though it was play, sometimes it awakened in him deep spiritual emotions which made him unconscious of the outer world. One day he lost himself so much in this mimic meditation in a secluded corner of the house that his relatives had to force open the door and shake him to bring him back to normal consciousness.

Naren had a fascination for wandering monks. Whenever a sadhu came to the door, Naren would be delighted and give him anything from the house as an offering. Naren would also have a peculiar experience when he would try to go to sleep. As soon as he closed his eyes there appeared between his eyebrows a wonderful spot of light of changing colours, which would expand and burst and bathe his whole body with a flood of white radiance. As the mind became preoccupied with this phenomenon, the body would fall asleep. It was a regular occurrence with him, and Narendra Nath thought this phenomenon was natural with everybody. But it indicated his great spiritual potentiality.

There was, however, another side of his character. As a child Narendra Nath was very naughty, and hard to manage. It needed two nurses to take care of him. He was of extraordinary restlessness and at times beyond control. Referring to this, his mother used to say, 'I prayed to Shiva for a son and He has sent me one of His demons.'

He was also a great tease. He would annoy his sisters and when chased would take refuge in the open drain, grinning and making faces at them in safety, for they would not follow him there. The family cow was one of his playmates, and he had a number of pet animals and birds, among which were a monkey, a goat, a peacock, pigeons, and two or three guinea-pigs. Of the servants the coachman was his special friend, and one of the ambitions of his childhood was to become a syce or groom. To him the syce with his turban and his whip, which he flourished as the carriage rolled on, was a magnificent person!

At the age of six Naren was sent to a primary school. At schools one is apt to meet with strange comrades, and after a few days he had acquired a vocabulary which quite upset the family's sense of propriety. So he was removed from the school, and a private tutor was engaged for him. Soon Naren showed remarkable intelligence in his studies. He learned to read and write while other boys were wrestling with the alphabet. His memory was prodigious. He had only to listen to the tutor's reading to learn the lessons. At the age of seven he knew by memory almost the whole of Mugdhabodha, a Sanskrit grammar, as well as passages of great length from the *Ramayana* and the *Mahabharata*.

When seven years old, Narendra joined the Metropolitan Institution founded by Pandit Ishwar Chandra Vidyasagar. His exceptional intelligence was at once recognized by teachers and class-mates. But he was so restless that, they say of him, he never really sat down at his desk at all.

Narendra was a favourite of his companions. He was always the leader among his friends. His favourite game was 'King and the Court'. The throne was the highest step of the stairs in a room. There he would install himself. No one was allowed to sit on the same level. From there he created his Prime Minister, Commander-in-Chief, Tributary Princes, and other state officials and seated them on steps according to their rank. He enacted a Durbar and administrated justice with royal dignity. The slightest insubordination was put down by a disapproving glare.

When he played, his play was lively. At the school, when the class was dispersed for lunch, he would be the first to finish and run back to the playground. New games always fascinated him, and he invented many to amuse himself and his friends. Disputes often arose among the boys, and it was to Naren that the disputants came as to a court of arbitration. Often he would turn the classroom into his playground. Even during the lessons he would entertain his friends with stories of the wild pranks he had played at home or with tales from the *Ramayana* or the *Mahabharata*.

Once during a lesson the teacher suddenly asked Naren and his friends, who were talking amongst themselves, to repeat what he had been saying. All were silent; but Naren, having the power to double his mind, was able to listen to the lesson, while he amused the boys. He answered correctly all the questions put to him. The teacher then asked who had been talking during the lesson, and would not believe the boys when they pointed to Naren. Teachers would often find it difficult to tackle such a student.

A Story is told of him showing how dauntless in spirit and impatient of superstition he was: Narendra Nath was in the habit of climbing a tree in the compound of one of his friends, not only to gather flowers, but to get rid of his superfluous energy by swinging to and fro, head downward, and then somersaulting to the ground. These antics annoyed the old, half-blind grandfather of the house, and he thought to stop them by telling Naren that the tree was haunted by an evil spirit that broke the necks of those who climbed the tree. Naren listened politely; but when the old man was out of sight, he again began to climb the tree. His friend who had taken the words of the old man seriously remonstrated. But Naren laughed at his seriousness and said, 'What an ass you are! Why, my neck would have been off long before this if the old grandfather's ghost story was true!'

Naren was the beloved of all. With every family in the locality, of high or low caste, rich or poor, he established some sort of relationship. If any of the boys whom he knew suffered any bereavement, he was the first to offer consolation. His ready wit and pranks kept everybody amused, sometimes, indeed, making even the grave-minded elders burst out into peals of laughter. He never suffered from shyness and he made himself at home everywhere.

Naren disliked monotony. He organized an amateur theatrical company and presented plays in the worship-hall of his home. Then he started a gymnasium in the courtyard of the house, where his friends used to take regular physical exercises. It went on for some time till one of his cousins broke his arm. Then it was stopped. Thereupon Naren joined the gymnasium of a neighbour with his friends and began to take lessons in fencing, lathiplay, wrestling, rowing, and other sports. Once he carried off the first prize in general athletic competition. When tired of these, he showed magic lantern pictures in his home.

At this time he conceived the idea of learning to cook, and he induced his playmates to subscribe according to their means towards the project, he himself, however, bearing the greater part of the expenses. He was the chief cook, and the others were his assistants.

Though the boy was full of wild pranks, he had no evil associate. His instinct kept him away from the dubious ways of the world. Truthfulness was the backbone of his life. Occupied during the day in games and various amusements, he was beginning to mediate during the night and soon was blessed with some wonderful vision. As Naren grew older, a definite change in his temperament was noticeable. He had a preference for intellectual pursuits, and he began to read books and newspapers, and to attend public lectures regularly. He was able to repeat the substance of these to his friends with such original criticism that they were astonished, and he developed an argumentative power which none could compete.

In the year 1877, while Naren was a student of the eighth class, his father went to Raipur in Madhya Pradesh. Naren also was taken there. There was no school in Raipur. This

2

gave Naren the time and opportunity to become
very intimate with his father—a great privilege,
for his father had a noble and cultured mind.
Vishwanath Datta attracted the intellect of his
son. He would hold long conversations with
him on topics that demanded depth, precision,
and soundness of thought. He gave the boy free
intellectual rein, believing that education is a
stimulus to thought and not a superimposition
of ideas. Many noted scholars visited Vishwanath. Naren would listen to their discussions,
and he occasionally joined in them. In these
days he demanded intellectual recognition from
everyone. So ambitious was he in this respect
that if his mental powers were not given
recognition, he would feel indignant and made
no secret about it. His father could not sanction
such outbursts and reprimanded the boy, but at
the same time in his heart he was proud of the
intellectual acumen and keen sense of self-
respect of his son.

Vishwanath Datta returned to Calcutta
with his family in 1879. There was some difficulty about getting Naren to school, for he had
been absent for two years. But his teachers
loved him and remembering his ability made an
exception in his case. Then he gave himself up
to study, mastering three years' lessons in one,

and passed the college Entrance Examination creditably.

At this time Naren made great progress in acquiring knowledge. Even while in the Entrance class he had mastered a great many standard works of English and Bengali literature and had read many books of history. He keenly studied standard works on Indian history. At this time he acquired a power of reading which he described as flowers: 'It so happened that I could understand an author without reading his book line by line. I could get the meaning by just reading the first and the last line of a paragraph. As this power developed, I found it unnecessary to read even the paragraphs. I could follow by reading only the first and last lines on a page. Further, where the author introduced discussion to explain a matter and it took him four or five or even more pages to clear the subject, I could grasp the whole trend of his argument by only reading the first few lines.'

After passing the Entrance Examination, Narendra Nath entered college. He first studied at the Presidency College, Calcutta, and then joined the General Assembly's Institution founded by the Scottish General Missionary Board. In college, he attracted the attention of both Indian and British professors, who were astounded by his brilliant intellect. Principal W.W. Hastie once said, 'I have travelled far and wide, but I have never yet come across a lad of his talents and possibilities. He is bound to make his mark in life.' Naren did not limit his studies to the curriculum. During the first two years of his college life he acquired a thorough grasp of all the masterpieces of Western logic, and in his third and fourth year classes he set himself to mastering Western philosophy as well as ancient and modern history of the different nations of Europe.

With all his seriousness there was another side to Naren. He had a great love for pleasure and gave himself up to it whole-heartedly. He was the soul of social circles, a brilliant conversationalist, a sweet singer, and the leader in all innocent fun. No party was complete without him. He was unconventional in manners and with flashes of keen wit would often expose all shows and mummeries of the world almost to the point of cynicism. He was as keen for adventure as ever and detested any sort of weakness. By far the most important trait in his character was purity. The opportunities for questionable adventures were many; but the influence of his mother made itself felt here, for

she had made purity a criterion of loyalty to
herself and family. Then, too, 'something'
always held him back, as he himself said later
on. He had a monastic instinct underneath the
surface of the frivolous life he seemed to live.
When his father began to urge him to marry,
with the tempting prospect of opportunities for
a good career, Naren rebelled. And strange to
say, every time the subject of marriage came up,
some unforeseen difficulty would arise, and the
matter would be abandoned.

MEETING WITH SRI RAMAKRISHNA

We have seen something of the religious disposition of Naren, his love for gods and goddesses, and his tendency to meditate. But as his intellectual horizon began to widen and he came more and more in contact with Western philosophy and science, Narendra Nath began to question his youthful theism and orthodox beliefs. Gradually his doubts and questionings took the form of an intellectual tempest which raged furiously and made him restless. He had faith and devotion, but he wanted reason to support them. At times he would think reason was the surest guide in life and reason could lead one to the realization of the ultimate Reality. But it was patent that a pale, bloodless reason could not satisfy human emotions, nor could it save one in the hour of trials and temptations. The study of John Stuart Mill, Hume, and Herbert Spencer raised a tumult of thoughts in him till his harassing doubts turned into a settled philosophical scepticism. But even in this, his innate religious nature gave him no rest. He longed for the Unknown, hungered for the realization of the Reality.

At this time the influence of the renowned Brahmo leader, Keshab Chandra Sen, over the young Bengali intellectuals was strong. Narendra Nath also was captivated by the lectures and writings of Keshab Chandra Sen. He began to interest himself in the Brahmo movement and actually became a member of the Sadharan Brahmo Samaj. The Brahmo movement protested against certain forms and tenets of the orthodox Hindu, such as polytheism, image worship, Divine Incarnation, and the need of a Guru (spiritual guide). It offered a monotheistic religion which repudiated all these. On the social side, it stood for reforms in the way of breaking up of the caste system and the caste consciousness, the recognition of the equality of man, the education and emancipation of women, and so on. It is not surprising that this movement captured the imagination of young Bengal. Naren came to regard the Samaj as an ideal institution in which might be solved all problems of life, individual and national. He chafed under the rigidity of caste and had no sympathy with polytheism and image worship. He espoused the cause with all earnestness and became imbued with the same ideas as the Brahmo leaders.

For a time the intellectual atmosphere of the Brahmo Samaj satisfied him; he felt uplifted during the prayer and devotional songs.

Gradually it began to dawn on him that, if God was to be realized, he was no nearer the goal than before he joined it. What were philosophies and Vedas but attempts to describe the Indescribable? They were useless if they did not bring one to the feet of the Lord!

In his longing to know the Truth he turned to Maharshi Devendra Nath Tagore, the Brahmo leader, who was regarded by many as one of the best of spiritual teachers. Tense with excitement, one day he approached him and burst out with the question: 'Sir, have you seen God?' The Maharshi was startled by such a question. Mad in his spiritual longing, Narendra Nath went to the leaders of other religious sects, but not one of them could satisfy him.

While Narendra Nath was thus suffering— his faith in Hinduism being undermined, and himself prey to the conflict of his own thoughts —there lived, four miles to the north of Calcutta, one whom people knew as Sri Ramakrishna and whose life was one long-drawn spiritual ecstasy—a bliss of the highest kind. The life of Sri Ramakrishna was just the antithesis of that of Narendra Nath. Sri Ramakrishna came of a poor, orthodox Brahmin family of a village in the district of Hooghly, where a ray of Western civilization had not reached. He had scarcely any secular learning and became a priest in the temple of Goddess Kali at Dakshineswar. Soon by his sincerity and intense Sadhana (spiritual endeavour) he realized a living presence in the image of Kali, who was now more than an earthly mother to him. Afterwards he performed spiritual practices as advocated by almost all schools of Hindu thought, and his life covered, as it were, the whole gamut of Hinduism. Not content with this he practised other religions also and came to the direct conclusion that all religions pointed to the same goal. Afterwards he lived a life more in tune with God than with the external world.

Narendra Nath once heard about Sri Ramakrishna from the principal of his college, William Hastie. One day Principal Hastie, while holding a class on Wordsworth, found it difficult to explain the ecstasy of the poet to his students. Then he said that for visual proof of such an experience one might go to Dakshineswar to see Ramakrishna, whom he had witnessed as enjoying that blessed state. Narendra Nath also once met Sri Ramakrishna at the house of a devotee in Calcutta, where Narendra Nath was invited to sing. Now, in his mental crisis, Narendra Nath suddenly remembered Sri Ramakrishna and decided to go to

Dakshineswar to find out if Sri Ramakrishna had the direct experience of God.

Narendra Nath went to Dakshineswar with some friends. Wrapped in his own thought, careless about his body and dress, and unmindful of the external world, Naren entered the room of Sri Ramakrishna. His eyes bespoke an introspective mind, as if some part of it were always concentrated upon something within. Sri Ramakrishna was surprised to find such a spiritual soul coming from the material atmosphere of Calcutta, as he said afterwards. Narendra Nath sang two Bengali songs at the request of Sri Ramakrishna. There was so much feeling and devotion in these songs that Sri Ramakrishna fell into Samadhi. After that Sri Ramakrishna beckoned Naren to go to the side room as if to give some private instructions. When Narendra Nath did so, Sri Ramakrishna began to shed tears of joy like one meeting a long-lost dear one. Then amidst sobs and with great tenderness Sri Ramakrishna began to tell how he was waiting for him for a long time, for his ears were well-nigh burnt in listening to the profane words of worldly people and he wanted the companionship of one who could appreciate his innermost experience. Narendra Nath was also told that he had a great spiritual mission to fulfil.

Narendra Nath was bewildered and thought Sri Ramakrishna must be a madman in talking that way. Before Sri Ramakrishna returned to his room, Narendra Nath promised that he would come again. In great amazement Narendra Nath came back to his friends. He now began to watch Sri Ramakrishna, and to his great surprise there was no strangeness in his behaviour. From his words and ecstatic states it transpired he was a genuine man of God. In the course of conversation Sri Ramakrishna said, 'God can be realized. One can see and talk to Him as I am doing with you. But who cares to do so?' There was so much ring of sincerity in these words that Narendra Nath could not disbelieve Sri Ramakrishna. It became apparent to him that these words came from the depth of his realization. But how to reconcile this with the strange conduct he had witnessed just now? Narendra Nath was in a great conflict. With utter confusion he returned to Calcutta. He could not decide whether Sri Ramakrishna was a monomaniac or not. But he could not deny that he was a great saint. He was at a loss to account for the strange feeling of blessedness that he experienced in the presence of Sri Ramakrishna. In spite of himself,

Narendra Nath was drawn to Sri Ramakrishna.

In about a month Narendra Nath once again set out for Dakshineswar, this time to encounter a stranger experience. Sri Ramakrishna received him very affectionately and called him to sit on the bed by his side. Then as Sri Ramakrishna in an ecstatic mood touched Narendra Nath, the latter became unconscious of the external world. To quote the words of Narendra Nath as he described the incident afterwards: 'The touch at once gave rise to a unique experience within me. With my eyes open I saw the walls and everything in the room whirl rapidly and vanish into naught, and the whole universe together with my individuality was about to merge in an all-encompassing mysterious Void! I was terribly frightened and thought I was facing death....Unable to control myself, I cried out, "What is this that you are doing to me? I have my parents at home!" He laughed aloud at this and stroking my breast said, "All right, let it rest now. Everything will come in time!" The wonder of it was that no sooner had he said this than that strange experience of mine vanished. I was myself again and found everything within and without the room as it had been before.'

This incident wounded the vanity of

Narendra Nath very much. He could not account for the fact that one, by mere touch, could revolutionize his mind. Was it mesmerism or hypnotism? It could be possible only with respect to weak minds. But Narendra Nath had so long prided himself on being just the reverse! This man could not be a lunatic as he thought him to be. Everything seemed like an enigma to him. The rationalistic mind of Narendra Nath received an unpleasant rebuff at this failure in judging the true state of things. In any case Narendra Nath was on guard to resist similar experiences. But at the same time he was fascinated by the remarkable personality of Sri Ramakrishna. He looked as pure and simple as a child! Narendra Nath was extremely drawn to him. So in about a week's time he came to Dakshineswar again.

But in the third visit Narendra Nath did no better, though he was on the defensive against any influence on the part of Sri Ramakrishna. This time Sri Ramakrishna took him to an adjacent garden and fell into ecstasy. In that state as he touched Narendra Nath, the latter, in spite of all precautions, was overwhelmed and lost all outward consciousness. When he came to himself he found Sri Ramakrishna stroking his chest.

Narendra had no idea of what had happened in the meantime. But it was then that Sri Ramakrishna learnt many things about him. Referring to this incident Sri Ramakrishna said later on that in that state as Narendra Nath dived deep into himself, Sri Ramakrishna studied his inner life, and the study only confirmed what he had inferred about his future disciple.

Narendra Nath was fully convinced of the extraordinary nature of that mighty power which was working through Sri Ramakrishna. The idea that Sri Ramakrishna was a monomaniac was replaced by a feeling of profound respect for him. He recognized Sri Ramakrishna as a great spiritual personality, but his mind was not fully prepared to accept him as a Guru. His mental make-up as well as his associations with the Brahmo Samaj prevented him from believing in the necessity of a Guru. How could a man, however great, be an unerring guide? So he would not accept any word of Sri Ramakrishna without testing it by his own experience or reason.

But Narendra Nath was conquered by the love of Sri Ramakrishna. He would now be coming to Dakshineswar as often as he could. Sri Ramakrishna also would be eagerly waiting for him. If Narendra Nath did not meet him for a long period, Sri Ramakrishna would pass sleepless nights. A mother suffering bereavement of her only child does not feel so much pang and anguish as Sri Ramakrishna did at the absence of Narendra Nath. And when Narendra Nath would come, at his very sight Sri Ramakrishna sometimes would go into ecstasy. There were many occasions when at the singing of Narendra Nath, Sri Ramakrishna would be lost in Samadhi.

Sri Ramakrishna saw the potential greatness of Narendra Nath. He was all praise for him. If other devotees could be likened to stars, Narendra Nath was a sun; if others were lotuses of six or ten or sixteen petals, Narendra Nath was a lotus of a thousand petals. Narendra Nath was a liberated soul from his very birth, born on this earth for the good of humanity. Often Sri Ramakrishna praised Narendra Nath so much that the latter had to remonstrate with him, saying that those conclusions were the outcome of his weak mind—a mind weakened by too much love for him.

With all his love for Sri Ramakrishna, Naren did not cease to wrestle with him. Naren did not believe in the need of a Guru, Naren did not believe in image worship, Naren did not believe in spiritual monism. Sri Ramakrishna had a hard time convincing his dear Naren about these. Sometimes exasperated, Sri Ramakrishna said to Narendra Nath, 'If you do not believe in my words, why do you come to me?' Immediately came the reply from Naren, 'Because I love you. But that does not mean that I shall accept your words without exercising my critical judgment.' Sri Ramakrishna only rejoiced at the intellectual sincerity of Narendra Nath. Of all the disciples Narendra Nath was the only one who would dare to challenge the very realizations of Sri Ramakrishna—so much so that at times Sri Ramakrishna had to go to the Divine Mother at the temple for a solution of the perplexity created in his mind by Narendra Nath. Naren would take the utmost liberty with Sri Ramakrishna. For others Sri Ramakrishna would prescribe this or that restriction as a spiritual guidance. But for Narendra Nath, there was no restriction whatsoever. Naren was a roaring fire. No impurity could touch him. He could not go wrong. So there was no necessity for any imposition on Narendra Nath.

It is very difficult to describe the sweet relationship that existed between Sri Ramakrishna and Narendra Nath. Sri Ramakrishna confided the innermost secrets of his heart to

Naren and helped him in a variety of ways to develop independence of thought, thus increasing thousandfold Naren's self-reliance, regard for truth, and innate spirituality. Naren's regard for Sri Ramakrishna also increased thousandfold as days rolled on, and he was beginning to accept him as the highest ideal of spirituality.

When Narendra Nath was dreaming of the fulfilment of his spiritual longing, an unexpected trouble came for him which upset him altogether. In the first part of 1884 Narendra Nath's father, who was the only support of the family, suddenly died of heart problems. He had spent more than he had earned, and at his death the family was faced with dire poverty. The creditors were knocking at the door. Narendra Nath's relatives, for whom his father had done so much, became enemies, even threatening to oust the family from the home. The burden of support of six or seven people, therefore, fell upon Narendra Nath. He had passed his B.A. Examination and was admitted to Law college. The son of a rich father, he was now the poorest of the poor in the college. Even shoes became a luxury, his garments were of the coarsest cloth, and many times he went to his classes hungry.

3

TRANSFORMATION

It was the abiding confidence of Sri Rama-krishna in the integrity of Naren's character as also the Master's selfless love for him that conquered his powerful heart. With the growing intimacy with the Master, Naren's tendency to resist lessened and eventually led to complete self-surrender. Afterwards Naren often said, 'Sri Ramakrishna was the only person who, ever since he had met me, believed in me uniformly throughout—even my mother and brothers did not do so. It was his unflinching trust and love for me that bound me to him for ever. He alone knew how to love another.'

With the ever increasing desire for illu-mination, the studies for the Law examination became a torment to Narendra Nath. His buoyant imagination which had already caught fire from the flame of his Master's spiritual life now refused to be satisfied with worldly aspira-tions. His soul wanted freedom from the galling fetters of existence. Very often, for the relaxation of his mental tension, he would run away from the stifling atmosphere of his home and take shelter at the feet of the Master in the holy temple-garden of Dakshineswar. The inner as-pirations of Naren's soul were fully visible to

the spiritually illumined vision of Sri Ramakrishna, who with infinite love and patience
began to train him. Naren, his gifted disciple,
was also astute enough to rise to his lofty
teaching, and with his brilliant intellect and
fiery enthusiasm was able to follow in life
whatever practical suggestion and words of
wisdom fell from the lips of the Master. He was
also the readiest among the disciples in arriving
at the true spirit of the Master's pregnant
gospel. One instance will suffice. One day, some
time during the year 1884, Sri Ramakrishna was
seated in his room at Dakshineswar surrounded
by his disciples. The conversation drifted to the
Vaishnava religion. The Master gave the gist of
the belief of some of its followers and finished
saying, 'This religion enjoins upon its followers
the practice of three things: relish for the name
of God, compassion for all living creatures and
service to the Vaishnavas—the devotees of the
Lord.' Hardly had he uttered these words when
he fell into Samadhi. After a while he came to a
semi-conscious state of mind and said to himself: 'Compassion for creatures! Compassion for
creatures! Thou fool! An insignificant worm
crawling on earth, thou to show compassion to
others! Who art thou to show compassion? No,
it cannot be. It is not compassion for others, but

rather service to man, recognizing him to be the veritable manifestation of God!'

Everyone present there, no doubt, heard those words of Sri Ramakrishna, but none but Naren could gauge their meaning. When Naren left the room he said to others, 'What a strange light have I discovered in those wonderful words of the Master! How beautifully has he reconciled the ideal of Bhakti (devotion) with the knowledge the Vedanta (non-dualism). I have understood from these words of wisdom that the ideal of Vedanta lived by the recluse outside the pale of society can be practised even from hearth and home and applied to all our daily schemes of life. Whatever may be the vocation of a man, let him understand and realize that it is God alone who has manifested Himself as the world and created beings. He is both immanent and transcendent. It is He who had become all diverse creatures, objects of our love, and yet He is beyond all these. Such realization of Divinity in humanity leaves no room for egotism. By realizing it, a man cannot have any jealousy or "pity" for any other being. Service of man, knowing him to be the manifestation of God, purifies the heart; and, in no time, such an aspirant realizes himself as part and parcel of God—Existence-Knowledge-Bliss

Absolute. However, if it be the will of the Lord, the day will soon come when I shall proclaim this grand truth before the world at large. I shall make it the common property of all, the wise and the fool, the rich and the poor, the Brahmin and the pariah.' In the fullness of time this high-souled desire of Narendra Nath came to be fulfilled to the letter and spirit. He proclaimed unto humanity this splendid ideal of service, based on knowledge, which he received as a sacred legacy from his Master in the serene peace of Dakshineswar.

It was in the middle of 1885 that Sri Ramakrishna showed the first symptom of throat trouble which ultimately ended in the fatal cancer. He was at first lodged in a house at Shyampukur for treatment and afterwards removed to a garden-house at Cossipore. The Master, knowing that he was approaching the end of his mortal existence, was eager to kindle in the heart of his chief disciples a burning desire for the realization of God. He not only imparted his spiritual instructions to his disciples, but he gave them likewise the stimulus and the strength to follow those teachings. His own life, the force of his utterances, the ease with which he entered into the highest Samadhi and his constant communion with the Divine—all these were a source of perennial inspiration to these young souls.

At the Cossipore garden Sri Ramakrishna was practically alone with his young disciples. Having given up their homes for the time at the urgent desire of Naren, they dedicated themselves in loving and devoted service to the Master. Naren was to them a constant source of inspiration. During their leisure periods, he would gather them together, and the time was spent in study, music, conversation, and discussions of the divine traits of their Master's character. Naren was the leader in every respect.

As the end of the Master came nearer, Narendra Nath's passionate desire for the realization of God increased and intensified. The Master would often send Naren and other disciples to meditate; and Naren, in the intensity of his meditations, became blessed with many rare spiritual experiences. The Master had already initiated him into various paths of spiritual discipline and was preparing him to be the head of the group of young monks who were to consecrate their lives in the near future to carrying out his mission. One day the Master expressly commissioned him to look after the young devotees, saying, 'I leave them to your care. See that they practise spiritual exercises even after my passing away and that they do not return home.' Another day, in preparation for the prospective monastic life, the Master commanded the young boys to beg their food from door to door as monks do. The food which they collected in this manner was cooked in the garden and offered to the Master, who was overjoyed. The Master knew that soon these young boys would put on the ochre robe of renunciation and go forth in quest of God, begging what food was necessary from householders. The Master himself initiated them as monks—thus fulfilling their heart's desire.

Now we come to the greatest moment of Naren's Sadhana, the very crest and glory of his spiritual realizations. Naren was pining for a vision of the Absolute. He prayed to feel Divinity. To lose the 'I' in the vastness of Consciousness which is beyond thought—was Narendra Nath's intense desire. Long did he pray to Sri Ramakrishna for this realization. One evening, however, it came unexpectedly. As he was meditating, he lost all body-consciousness and his mind plunged into the superconscious state. It was a state of Nirvikalpa Samadhi.

Referring to this incident Sri Ramakrishna

said afterwards, 'I have prayed that the Divine
Mother may keep this realization of the
Absolute veiled from Naren. There is much
work to be done by him. But this veil is so very
thin that it may give way at any time.' It was
because of Naren's intense desire to realize the
Absolute Brahman that Sri Ramakrishna
decided to give that experience to him. But the
Master had no intention of permitting him to
stay there, since much work was waiting for
Narendra Nath. Three or four days before his
passing away, Sri Ramakrishna called Naren
near and actually commissioned him for future
work.

It was on August 16, 1886, that Sri Ramakrishna passed away leaving his disciples in
deep gloom. After the death of the Master,
Naren began to organize these disciples into a
monastic brotherhood. He went to the homes of
those boys who had resumed their studies, and,
by a whirlwind of enthusiasm, tried to induce
them to return to Baranagore where the first
monastery of the Ramakrishna Order was
started. Once at the monastery, they could not
resist the spiritual impetus of Naren's songs and
thrilling conversations. One by one the young
disciples joined together and ultimately banded
themselves into a holy brotherhood under the

inspiring leadership of Narendra Nath. The boys were now in the midst of extreme privations. They were so determined in their desire to follow the injunctions of the Master that, forgetting sleep, they spent night after night in prayer and spiritual exercises. Naren always spurred them on to burning renunciation and intense devotion. Hours were also consumed in the study of philosophy, both Eastern and Western, to intensify their struggle for the realization of the highest Truth. All who came within the sphere of their influence were also caught up in their spirit of God-intoxication. With the delight of a martyr these monks practised the severest of spiritual austerities, and the world had no meaning for them at that time. Some time during this period they performed the sacred Viraja ceremony and formally took the vows of lifelong celibacy and poverty, dedicating their lives to the realization of God. The old names were changed for new ones to complete their severance from their earlier life and its associations.

A WANDERING MONK

Soon a tendency to embrace a wandering life, according to the traditions of monks, was most irresistibly felt by most of these young monks. Naren, in spite of his anxiety to maintain the ties of uniting the brotherhood, was himself tormented with the same desire to strike out into the unknown paths of the monks' life and to lose himself in the silence of the wild, under the wide canopy of heavens. Naren resisted the call to flight for two years, and apart from his short visits to some neighbouring places, he practically remained at Baranagore until 1888. But he was determined to break away from the monastery to test his own strength, to gather experiences of a new life, to make himself absolutely fearless, and at the same time to force his brother-disciples to learn self-reliance and to stand alone. He therefore suddenly left Calcutta in 1888 and went to Varanasi, Ayodhya, Lucknow, Agra, Vrindaban, Hathras, and the Himalayas. At the railway station of Hathras he quite unintentionally made Sharat Chandra Gupta, the station-master, his disciple, who afterwards took the name of Sadananda. Sharat Chandra, without a moment's hesitation, left his hearth and home and followed the Swami gladly in his itinerary through the hills. For some time both were lost in the silence of the Himalayas and were almost dead to the outside world. But physical hardship and severe spiritual austerities undermined their health, and both had to come back to the Baranagore monastery after gathering manifold experiences.

After a year the Swami again went out and visited, among other places, Ghazipur. During his stay at Ghazipur, he met the illustrious saint Pavhari Baba who had attained to great spiritual heights through hard austerities and Yogic practices. Despite the useful lessons which he was able to gather from his travels, his heart still panted for a life of absolute freedom from all external trammels. He wanted to plunge into the depths of the Himalayas to acquire through extreme forms of mental discipline a tremendous spiritual power which would enable him to carry on his Master's mission without let or hindrance. With this end in view he broke loose at the beginning of July 1890, this time for many years, from the Baranagore monastery. Swami Akhandananda, one of his brother-disciples, who had just returned from his Tibetan travels with a fund of wonderful experiences of the life and manners of the people of the Himalayas, became his companion. At Varanasi the Swami wrote to his friend, Pramadadas Mitra, a great Sanskrit scholar, 'I am going away; but I shall never come back until I can burst on society like a bomb, and make it follow me like a dog.' From the moment he left Calcutta he was happy. The solitude, the village air, the sight of new places, the meeting with new people and getting rid of old impressions and worry delighted him. When they reached the Himalayas, the splendid scenery with its waterfalls, streams, wild forests, and its serenity and quietude and, above all, its invigorating atmosphere buoyed up the spirit of the Swami, and the occasional glimpses of the eternal snows filled his heart with unspeakable emotion and joy. They wanted to go to Kedarnath and Badrikashrama, but they had to give up their idea of visiting those ancient places of pilgrimage as the road was closed by the Government on account of famine.

By February 1891, the Swami finally became a solitary monk and began his historic wandering of two years through India. He wandered, free from any plan, constantly with the thought of God in his mind. The Swami, in the course of his pilgrimage around India, met with all sorts and conditions of men and found himself—today a despised beggar sheltered by pariahs or a brother of the oppressed identifying himself in keen sympathy with their misery, and tomorrow a guest of the princes, conversing on equal terms with Prime Ministers and Maharajas and probing the luxury of the great, and awakening care for the public weal in their torpid hearts.

First he visited Rajputana, the land of heroes, where he met some of the most enlightened princes of the day. While at Alwar the Swami had a very interesting discussion with Prince Mangal Singh. The Maharaja asked the Swami, 'Well, I have no faith in idol worship. I cannot worship wood, earth, stone, or metal, like other people. Does this mean that I shall fare worse in the life hereafter?' The eyes of the Swami alighted on a picture of the Maharaja which was hanging on the wall. At his express desire it was passed to him. Holding it in his hand, the Swami asked, 'Whose picture is this?' The Dewan answered, 'It is the likeness of our Maharaja.' A moment later those present trembled with fear when they heard the Swami commanding the Dewan to spit on it. The Dewan was thunderstruck, and the eyes of all glanced in terror and awe from the Prince to the monk, from the monk to the Prince. But all the while the Swami insisted, 'Spit on it! I say, spit on it!' And the Dewan in fear and bewilderment cried out, 'What! Swamiji! What are you asking me to do? This is the likeness of our Maharaja. How can I do such a thing?' 'Be it so,' said the Swami, 'but the Maharaja is not bodily present in this photograph. This is only a piece of paper. It does not contain his bones and flesh and blood. It does not speak or behave or move in any way as does the Maharaja. And yet all of you refuse to spit on it, because you see in this photo the shadow of the Maharaja's form. Indeed, in spitting upon the photo, you feel that you insult your master, the Prince himself.' Turning to the Maharaja, he continued: 'See, Your Highness, though this is not you in one sense, in another sense it is you. That was why your devoted servants were so perplexed when I asked them to spit upon it. It has a shadow of you; it brings you into their minds. One glance at it makes them see you in it! Therefore they look upon it with as much respect as they do upon your own person. Thus it is with the devotees who worship stone and metal images of gods and goddesses. It is because an image brings to their minds their Ishta (chosen deity), or some special form and attribute of the Divinity, and helps them to concentrate, that the devotees worship God in an image. They do not worship the stone or the metal as such. Everyone, O Maharaja, is worshipping the same one God who is the Supreme Spirit, the Soul of Pure Knowledge. And God appears to all according to their understanding and their representation of Him.' The Maharaja who had been listening attentively all this time said with folded hands: 'Swamiji! I must admit that according to the light you have thrown upon image worship, I have never yet met anyone who had worshipped stone, or wood, or metal. Heretofore I did not understand its meaning. You have opened my eyes.'

This is but one of the numerous instances to show what illuminating discourses the Swami had, in the course of his tour, with men of learning and influence, and how, with his characteristic frankness and boldness, he told all whatever he felt to be true and proper in the inmost core of his heart. But occasions were not wanting when the Swami learnt lessons of the highest wisdom even from the lowliest and the lost. One instance would suffice. Just before the Swami's departure for the West, the Maharaja of Khetri, who had already become his initiated disciple, accompanied the Swami as far as Jaipur. On this occasion the Maharaja was being

entertained one evening with music by a
nautch-girl. The Swami was in his own tent
when the music commenced. The Maharaja sent
a message to the Swami asking him to come
and join the party. The Swami sent word in
return that as a Sannyasin he could not comply
with such a request. The singer was deeply
grieved when she heard this, and sang in reply,
as it were, a song of the great Vaishnava saint,
Surdas. Through the still evening air, to the
accompaniment of music, the girl's melodious
voice ascended to the ears of the Swami—

'O Lord, look not upon my evil qualities!
Thy name O Lord, is Same-sightedness.
One piece of iron is in the image in the temple,
And another is the knife in the hand of the
        butcher;
But when they touch the philosophers' stone,
Both alike turn to gold.
So, O Lord, look not upon my evil qualities!
One drop of water is in the sacred Jumna,
And another is foul in the ditch by the roadside;
But when they fall into the Ganga
Both alike become holy.
So, Lord, do not look upon my evil qualities!
Thy name, O Lord, is Same-sightedness.'

The Swami was completely overwhelmed. The woman and her meaningful song at once reminded him that the same Divinity dwells in the high and the low, the rich and the poor—in the entire creation. The Swami could no longer resist the request, and took his seat in the hall of audience to meet the wishes of the Maharaja. Speaking of this incident later, the Swami said, 'That incident removed the scales from my eyes. Seeing that all are indeed the manifestations of the One, I could no longer condemn anybody.'

The Swami's itineracy led him through almost all the historic places of Rajputana, Bombay State, and Southern India till at last he reached Kanyakumari in all probability on 23 December 1892. No doubt, every moment of these travels of his with an open mind for several years throughout the length and breadth of India—from the dreamy poetic regions of the snow-capped Himalayas down to Kanyakumari, the last promontory of the land where the mighty ocean spreads out into infinity—were eventful. All this wandering had a great educational value for him, opening up, as it did, opportunities for original thought and observation, the most striking element in all of which was his tireless search for unity in the world of Indian ideals. Nevertheless, it was at Kanya-

kumari that his pilgrimage throughout his
motherland, and his days and months of
thought on the problem of the Indian masses
bore fruit.

Happy as a child is to be back with its
mother, so was the Swami when he prostrated
before the image of the Divine Mother in the
seashore temple at Kanyakumari. After worshipping the Mother, he swam across some two fur-
longs of the shark-infested ocean and reached
the farther of the two rocks that form the
southernmost extremity of India. Over the three
days he sat there, he was in a long and deep
meditation. The Swami himself has told of the
thoughts that moved through his mind during
that period. He saw, as it were, the whole of
India—her past, present, and future, her centuries of greatness and also her centuries of
degradation. He saw that it was not religion
that was the cause of India's downfall but, on
the contrary, the fact that her true religion, the
very life and breath of her individuality, was
scarcely to be found, and he knew that her only
hope was a renascence of the lost spiritual
culture of the ancient rishis. His mind encom-
passing both the roots and the ramifications of
India's problem, and his heart suffering for his
country's downtrodden, poverty-stricken

masses, he 'hit', as he later wrote, 'upon a plan.

> We are so many sannyasins wandering about and teaching the people metaphysics—it is all madness. Did not our Gurudeva use to say, 'An empty stomach is no good for religion'? That those poor people are leading the life of brutes is simply due to ignorance. We have for all ages been sucking their blood and trampling them under foot.
>
> …Suppose some disinterested sannyasins, bent on doing good to others, go from village to village, disseminating education, and seeking in various ways to better the condition of all down to the Chandala, through oral teaching, and by means of maps, cameras, globes, and other accessories—can't that bring forth good in time? All these plans I cannot write out in this short letter. The long and short of it is—if the mountain does not come to Mohammed, Mohammed must go to the mountain. The poor are too poor to come to schools,…and they will gain nothing by reading poetry and all that sort of thing. We as a nation have lost our individuality, and that is the cause of all mischief in

India. We have to give back to the nation
its lost individuality and *raise the masses*.
The Hindu, the Mohammedan, the Christian, all have trampled them under foot.
Again, the force to raise them must come
from inside, that is, from the orthodox
Hindus. In every country the evils exist not
with, but against religion. Religion therefore is not to blame, but men.

To effect this, the first thing we need
is men, and the next is funds.

And that is why, in the presence of the
Maharaja of Mysore, the Swami burst forth into
an eloquent description of what was prompting
him to go the West.[1] He told the Maharaja that
he intended to go to America to ask the West
for the means to ameliorate the material
condition of India and to take to it in exchange
the gospel of Vedanta.

The Swami again spoke of the same
mission when he met by chance two of his
brother-disciples, Swamis Brahmananda and
Turiyananda, at the Abu Road train station. To
them he said with a pathetic appeal, 'I have

1. The Swami was thinking of attending the Parliament
of Religions which, he had already heard at Khandwa,
was to be held at Chicago in America in 1893.

travelled all over India. But alas, it was agony to me, my brothers, to see with my own eyes the terrible poverty and misery of the masses, and I could not restrain my tears! It is now my firm conviction that it is futile to preach religion amongst them without first trying to remove their poverty and their suffering. It is for this reason—to find more means for the salvation of the poor of India—that I am now going to America.' Of this meeting with the Swami at the above station, Swami Turiyananda said later on, 'I vividly remember some remarks made by Swamiji at that time. The accents and deep pathos with which they were uttered still ring in my ears. He said, "Haribhai, I am still unable to understand anything of your so-called religion." Then with an expression of deep sorrow in his countenance and an intense emotion shaking his body, he placed his hand on his heart and added: "But my heart has expanded very much, and I have learnt to feel. Believe me, I feel intensely indeed." His voice was choked with feeling; he could say no more. For a time, profound silence reigned and tears rolled down his cheeks.' In telling of this incident Swami Turiyananda was also overcome with deep emotion. With a heavy sigh he said, 'Can you imagine what passed through my mind on hearing the Swami speak thus? "Are not these," I thought, "the very words and feelings of Buddha?"...I could clearly perceive that the sufferings of humanity were pulsating in the heart of Swamiji—his heart was a huge cauldron in which the sufferings of mankind were being made into a healing balm. Nobody could understand Vivekananda unless he saw at least a fraction of the volcanic feelings which were in him.'

The Swami next journeyed from Kanya-kumari to Rameswaram during the last days of 1892, and from there to Madras at the beginning of 1893. From the day of his arrival there he was besieged with numerous visitors and he seemed to be on the road to public recognition. It was in Madras that the message of the Master gained a ready acceptance, and a brilliant group of enthusiastic young men became his ardent adherents. It was here that his intention to attend the Parliament of Religions took a definite shape. During the months of March and April, 1893, the disciples of the Swami took active steps to raise requisite funds for this purpose. But before leaving for America, the Swami had to visit Khetri at the earnest importunities of the Maharaja, his disciple. It was at the court of the Maharaja of Khetri that the

Swami, at the Maharaja's request, assumed the name of Vivekananda by which he was to be known in future. He sailed from Bombay on May 31, 1893—a memorable day for India.

FROM THE OLD WORLD TO THE NEW

Swami Vivekananda went by way of Ceylon, Penang, Singapore, Hongkong, and then visited Canton and Nagasaki. From there he went by land to Yokohama, seeing Osaka, Kyoto, and Tokyo. The Swami gradually accustomed himself to the life on board the ship. His rich imaginative nature saw beauty, in a thousand forms, in the swelling and falling of the waters, in every gust of wind and in ever-changing shapes of clouds. The mighty expanse of water, the invigorating air, the carefree atmosphere and the courtesy of all aboard reconciled him to his new surroundings. Besides, the sea voyage provided him a unique opportunity to gather new experiences and study the life and traditions of the people he came in contact with at different places. He was much impressed at the sight of the various remains of Indian religious influences in Chinese and Japanese temples. In China he found to his amazement Sanskrit manuscripts, and in Japan Sanskrit Mantras written in old Bengali script. In fact, everywhere in China and Japan his attention was attracted by all that might confirm his hypothesis alike of the

station he found to his dismay that he had lost the address of the Committee. He was lost and did not know where to go. Nobody would deign to inform a coloured man. At length, tired and helpless, he passed the chilly night in a big empty box[2] found in the railway freightyard. In the morning he wandered from door to door for food only to meet with insults and rebuffs from the fashionable residents of the metropolis. On and on he went. At length exhausted, he sat down quietly on the roadside, determined to abide by the Will of God. At this juncture, the door of a fashionable residence opposite to him opened and a regal looking woman descended and accosted him in a soft voice in accents of culture and refinement, 'Sir, are you a delegate to the Parliament of Religions?' The Swami told her his difficulties. The kind-hearted lady invited him into her house and promised him that after breakfast she herself would accompany him to the offices of the Parliament of Religions. The Swami was grateful beyond words to his deliverer, Mrs. George W. Hale. From now on the generous lady, her husband and children became his dearest friends.

With Mrs. Hale he called on the officers of

---

2. Probably a boxcar, or a railway wagon.

the Parliament, gave his credentials, was gladly accepted as a delegate, and found himself lodged with the other Oriental delegates. He soon made acquaintance with many distinguished personages who were to attend the Parliament. In the grand circle of ecclesiastics that came and went in and about Chicago, he moved as one lost in rapture and in prayer to the Master whose mission he had come to fulfil in this distant part of the world.

Vivekananda as a Wandering Monk

IN THE PARLIAMENT OF
RELIGIONS

On Monday, September 11, 1893, the first session of the Parliament was opened in the great Hall of Columbus, where were seated representatives of the religious beliefs of twelve hundred millions of the human race. In the centre sat Cardinal Gibbons, the highest prelate of the Roman Catholic Church on the Western Continent. On the right and left of him were gathered the Oriental delegates—Pratap Chandra Majumdar of Bengal and Nagarkar of Bombay who were representatives of the Brahmo Samaj; Dharmapala who represented the Buddhists of Ceylon; Gandhi (a distant relation of Mahatma Gandhi) representing the Jains, and Mr. Chakravarty representing Theosophy with Mrs. Annie Besant. Among them was also seated Swami Vivekananda who, with his noble bearing, bright countenance and gorgeous apparel, drew the attention of the assembled thousands and soon became the cynosure of all eyes. It was the first time that he had to speak before such an august assembly; and as the delegates, presented one by one, had to announce themselves in public in brief speeches, the Swami let his turn go by hour after hour until the end of the day.

At length, in the late afternoon, when the Chairman insisted, the Swami rose and bowed down to Saraswati, the Goddess of Learning. His face glowed like fire. His eyes surveyed in a sweep the huge assembly before him. When he opened his lips, his speech was like a tongue of flame. Hardly had he pronounced the very simple opening words, 'Sisters and Brothers of America', when hundreds rose to their feet with deafening shouts of applause. The Parliament had gone mad—everyone cheering the Swami enthusiastically. For two minutes he attempted to speak, but the wave of wild enthusiasm created by this significant form of address prevented it. He was certainly the first to cast off the formalism of the Congress and speak to the audience in the language for which they were waiting. When silence was restored, the Swami greeted the youngest of the nations in the name of the most ancient order of monks in the world—the Vedic order of Sannyasins, and presented Hinduism as the mother of religions —a religion which had taught the world both tolerance and universal acceptance. He quoted two beautiful, illustrative passages taken from the scriptures of Hinduism:

'As the different streams having their

sources in different places all mingle their water in the sea, so O Lord, the different paths which men take, through different tendencies, various though they may appear, crooked or straight, all lead to Thee.'

'Whosoever comes to Me, through what-soever form, I reach him; all men are struggling through paths which in the end lead to Me.'

It was only a short speech, but its spirit of universality, its fundamental earnestness and broadmindedness completely captivated the whole assembly. There were other Hindu deleg-ates who stood for societies or churches or sects, but the Swami, who belonged to no sect but rather to India as a whole, proclaimed the uni-versality of religious truths and the sameness of the Goal of all religious realizations. In the course of his illuminating addresses during the sessions of the Parliament, the Swami placed before the distinguished audience the cardinal truths of Vedanta, the universal religion of humanity.

He said: 'If there is ever to be a universal religion, it must be one which will have no location in place or time; which will be infinite, like the God it will preach, and whose sun will shine upon the followers of Krishna and Christ, on saint and sinners alike; which will not be

Brahminic or Buddhistic, Christian or Mohammedan, but the sum total of all these, and still have infinite space for development; which in its catholicity will find a place for every human being, from the lowest grovelling savage not far removed from the brute to the highest man towering by the virtues of his head and heart almost above humanity. It will be a religion which will have no place for persecution or intolerance in its polity, which will recognize divinity in every man and woman, and whose whole scope, whose whole force, will be centred in aiding humanity to realize its own true, divine nature. Offer such a religion and all the nations will follow you.... The Christian is not to become a Hindu or a Buddhist, nor a Hindu or a Buddhist to become a Christian. But each must assimilate the spirit of the others and yet preserve his individuality and grow according to his own law of growth.'

The Parliament of Religions, he concluded, had shown to the world that holiness, purity, and charity were not the exclusive possession of any church in the world and that every system had produced men and women of the most exalted character. In the face of this evidence, if anybody dreamt of the exclusive survival of his own religion and the destruction of others, he

5

was to be pitied and told that upon the banner of every religion will soon be written, in spite of resistance: 'Help and not fight,' 'Assimilation and not Destruction', 'Harmony and Peace and not Dissension'.

The effect of these mighty words was tremendous. Over the heads of the official representatives of the Parliament they were addressed to a wider public, and Swami Vivekananda at once became the most celebrated personality of the Parliament. The American press rang with his fame. The best known and most conservative of the metropolitan newspapers proclaimed him a Prophet and a Seer. *The New York Herald* referred to him as 'undoubtedly the greatest figure in the Parliament of Religions', and added, 'After hearing him we feel how foolish it is to send missionaries to this learned nation.'

The news of Swami Vivekananda's unparalleled success soon poured into India as well. Indian journals and magazines—from Madras to Almora, from Calcutta to Bombay—were filled with the American reports of his triumph at the Parliament. The happiness of the monks of the Ramakrishna Order at Baranagore knew no bounds when they came to learn that it was their beloved leader who had taken the New

World by storm. The citizens of Calcutta organized a great representative meeting in the Town Hall to thank the Swami and the American people. The name Vivekananda rang with acclaim throughout the length and breadth of Hindusthan. Everywhere he was recognized as the man who had come to fulfil a great need. The unknown monk without titles and ties blossomed into a world-figure and became the man of the hour.

But in the midst of this recognition of his genius, universal applause, and immense popularity, the Swami was never found for a moment forgetful of his duties to the sunken masses of India. On the very day of his triumph when he was invited by a man of great wealth and distinction to his home and lodged in a princely room fitted with luxury beyond anything he could conceive, instead of feeling happy in this splendid environment he was miserable. He could not sleep, pondering, in contrast, over India's plight. The bed of down became to him a bed of thorns. He rolled down on the empty floor and in agony of his heart cried, 'O Mother, what do I care for name and fame when my motherland remains sunk in utmost poverty? Who will raise the masses in India? Who will give them bread? Show me, O

Mother, how I can help them.' He wrote inspiring letters to his disciples and admirers in India to stimulate their hearts into activity and a high pitch of patriotic fervour. 'Gird up your loins, my boys,' he once wrote, 'I am called by the Lord for this. The hope lies in you—in the meek, the lowly, but the faithful. Feel for the miserable and look up for help—it shall come. With a bleeding heart I have crossed half the world to this strange land seeking for help. The Lord will help me. I may perish of cold and hunger in this land, but I bequeath to you, young men, this sympathy, this struggle for the poor, the ignorant, the oppressed. Go down on your faces before Him and make a great sacrifice, the sacrifice of a whole life for them—these three hundred millions, going down and down every day. Glory unto the Lord, we will succeed. Hundreds will fall in the struggle— hundreds will be ready to take it up. Life is nothing, death is nothing. Glory unto the Lord—march on, the Lord is our General. Do not look back to see who falls—forward, onward!'

The Swami never forgot in the midst of luxury the primary idea of his mission—to save his people, to mobilize them to help him in his task by widening his appeal until it became the cause of the people, the cause of the poor and the oppressed of the whole world.

In order to serve the cause of his motherland he accepted the offer of a lecture bureau for a tour of the United States. In the course of this apostolic campaign in America he began to tell of the glories of India and the greatness of Indian culture and spirituality.

AS A TEACHER IN AMERICA

The Swami, finding that the lecture bureau was exploiting and defrauding him, soon shook himself free from American lecturing organizations. At the beginning of the winter of 1894, he returned to New York after a whirlwind tour through various centres of learning and culture in America. His previous visits to this noted city had been only casual. He had given only a few public lectures but was not in a position to begin any constructive work. With a view to starting regular work the Swami now readily accepted the invitation of the Brooklyn Ethical Association to deliver a series of lectures. These lectures produced the desired effect and opened a new avenue for organizing the work in America. He soon found a group of earnest souls who were seriously bent on following the guidance of the Swami for spiritual enlightenment. The Swami gave his whole time to teaching by means of talks and lectures, and every day instructed this band of chosen followers in the exercise of the double method of Raja-Yoga and Jnana-Yoga. His lectures at this time were replete with the deepest philosophical insight and with extraordinary outbursts of devotion, revealing his nature as essentially a combination of the Jnani and Bhakta—the illumined saint and true mystic in one.

Prominent among those who became his ardent followers at this time were Mrs. Ole Bull, Dr. Day, Miss S.E. Waldo, Professors Wyman and Wright, Dr. Street, and many clergymen and laymen of note. Mr. and Mrs. Francis Leggett and Miss MacLeod, well-known society people of New York, became his most intimate friends. By the month of June 1895, the Swami had placed his real constructive work on a solid foundation, and also finished writing his famous treatise on Raja-Yoga, dictated to Miss S.E. Waldo (afterwards Sister Haridasi), which soon attracted the attention of American psychologists like William James. The Swami also had support from wealthy and influential followers, and whatever he could save from the financial returns he received went towards further consolidation of his work. All through the year the Swami's work was enormous; he was working intensely; lecturing both privately and publicly, he began to feel himself wearing out. But the Swami was satisfied that the ideals of the Sanatana Dharma, the Eternal Religion, were spreading and percolating through the whole thought-world of America, and that they were very often echoed in pulpits and in rostrums, though it might be that he received no credit for them.

Having almost exhausted himself by this uninterrupted work of class and public lecturing, the Swami now eagerly sought a place of retreat where he could give a modicum of rest to his shattered nerves and train up a group of students for future action. One of the students, Miss Dutcher, owned a handsome cottage at Thousand Island Park, the largest island in the St. Lawrence River and she offered the use of it to the Swami and as many of the students as it would accommodate. The place was ideally situated, overlooking a wide sweep of the beautiful river with many of its far-famed Thousand Islands. Not a human sound penetrated the seclusion of the house. The inmates heard but the murmur of the insects, the sweet songs of the birds, or the gentle sighing of the wind through the leaves. Part of the time the scene was illumined by the soft rays of the moon and her face was mirrored in the shining waters beneath.

In this scene of enchantment, the devoted students spent seven blessed weeks with their beloved teacher, listening to his words of inspiration. This group of twelve included, Miss S.E. Waldo and Miss Greenstidel who later became Sister Christine and ably assisted Sister Nivedita in her educational work in India.

During the Swami's stay in this island he threw light upon all manner of subjects, historical and philosophical, spiritual and temporal. It was as if the contents of his nature were pouring themselves forth as a grand revelation of the many-sidedness of the Eternal Truth. Certainly the seven weeks lived at Thousand Island Park were one of the freest and the greatest periods in the Swami's life. Surrounded by ardent disciples he was there in the uninterrupted stillness of the island retreat, in an atmosphere reminiscent of that in which his Master had lived and taught in the Dakshineswar days of old. The whirlwind of spiritual rhapsody and ecstasy that had swept the souls of devotees in Dakshineswar on the bank of the Ganga, swept here anew the souls of other devotees in this lonely region. Some glimpses of his ecstatic utterances of this period can be had in *Inspired Talks*, a book which owes not a little to the sedulous care and industry of Miss Waldo, one of this enthusiastic group of students on the island. It was in the silence of this retreat that the Swami wrote also the immortal *Song of the Sannyasin*, which has now become one of the most precious legacies to spiritually-minded souls.

Having fulfilled his great work of training and initiating disciples into Brahmacharya and Sannyasa at Thousand Island Park, the Swami returned to New York, from where he soon sailed to England to carry to the British people the same message which he had preached in America. During his absence the work of spreading Vedanta was carried on uninterrupted by the group of his trained disciples. But the Swami's presence was greatly needed in the New World for the consolidation of the various work started there. So he soon returned.

With a view to giving a concrete shape to his Vedantic work on the American soil, the Swami after the close of his public lectures in the latter part of February 1896, organized the Vedanta movement into a definite society and began to issue his teachings in book form. Thus came into existence The Vedanta Society of New York, a non-sectarian body with the aim of preaching and practising Vedanta and applying its principles to all faiths. Its members met regularly at appointed times for the purpose of carrying on co-operative and organized work, and for the study and propaganda of Vedanta literature. Some of the great works like *Raja-Yoga*, *Bhakti-Yoga*, and *Karma-Yoga* had already been published and aroused a interest among some of the great savants and thinkers of America.

One of the principal purposes of the Swami in organizing his classes into this Society was particularly to bring about an interchange of ideas and ideals between the East and the West. Already he had in his mind the plan of bringing from India some of his brother-disciples to teach and preach in America, and also of having some of his American, and English disciples in India to teach and preach there. In America it would be religious teaching, and in India it would be practical training—a message of science, industry, economics, applied sociology, organization, and co-operation. The Indian needed that energy, that dexterity in action, that thirst for improvement which characterized the freedom-loving people of the active West. In the opinion of the Swami, the Orient would be benefited by greater activity and energy like that of the West, as the latter would profit by a mixture of Eastern introspection and the meditative habit. The Swami made Mr. Francis H. Leggett, one of the wealthy and influential residents of the city of New York, the President of this newly formed Vedanta Society.

The universal teachings and profound

learning of the Swami made a deep impression upon the minds of the American intelligentsia. He was even offered the Chair of Oriental Philosophy at Harvard university and at Columbia the Chair of Sanskrit. Besides the distinguished psychologists and philosophers, influential persons of other fields of thought also were charmed with his erudition and knowledge of science and arts. The fearless outspokenness of the Swami often alienated that general approval for which so many public workers slave and sacrifice their true views and their principles. But, after all, he found that the American public, though at first it might appear to resent, would afterwards regard with great admiration one who dared to speak openly of what he felt were the drawbacks of its civilization. At the end of his American work the Swami was thoroughly tired. Everything he did, said, or wrote was at the white heat of intensity; and this undoubtedly undermined even his strong constitution. His friends knew that he had given himself wholly and unstintedly for the good of those who made his message the gospel of their lives.

IN ENGLAND

We have already seen that Swami Vivekananda, after closing his teaching work in Thousand Island Park, visited England in the latter part of 1895. As a matter of fact, he made three visits there; from September to the end of November 1895; from April to the end of July 1896; and from October to December 16, 1896. From the moment he set foot in England he breathed a quite different atmosphere of culture and tradition. He discovered here a nation of heroes, brave and steady. But while he admired the English people, he never lost sight of his Indian mission. He once wrote to Mr. Leggett in America, 'The British Empire with all its drawbacks is the greatest machine that ever existed for the dissemination of ideas. I mean to put my ideas in the centre of this machine, and they will spread all over the world.' On the way the Swami visited Paris, the centre of European culture, and was delighted to see the museums, churches, cathedrals, art galleries, and other artistic wealth of the nation. He was introduced in Paris to some of the enlightened friends of his host, with whom he discoursed on subjects which ranged from the most learned studies to the highest spiritual thoughts.

On his arrival in England, Swami Vivekananda was warmly received by friends, among
them being Miss Henrietta Müller, who had
already met him in America, and Mr. E.T.
Sturdy. After a few days rest he commenced
work in a quiet way. During the day he paid
visits to every place of historic or artistic
interest; in the mornings, and often in the late
evenings, he held classes and gave interviews.
His reputation spread at once, and within three
weeks of his arrival he found himself engaged
in strenuous activity. The Press welcomed and
heralded his ideas, and some of the most select
clubs of the city of London and even some
leaders of its prominent clerical institutions
invited him and received him with marked admiration. He was moving in the best circles of
English society, and even members of the
nobility were glad to recognize him as their
friend. This completely revolutionized the
Swami's idea of Englishmen and women. In
America he found that the public was most
enthusiastic and responsive in taking up new
ideas; but in England he discovered that,
though his hearers were more conservative in
their praise and declaration of acceptance, they
were all the more fervent and staunch, once
they had convinced themselves of the worth of

a teacher and his ideas.

Though his stay in London was very short this time, he had the joyous satisfaction of being able to count many as his sincere friends and earnest supporters. Among these was Miss Margaret Noble (afterwards Sister Nivedita) who was the headmistress of an educational institution and a conspicuous member of the Sesame Club, founded for the furtherance of educational purposes. She moved in quiet but distinguished intellectual circles and was deeply interested in all modern influences and thought. She was struck with the novelty and the breadth of the Swami's religious culture and the intellectual freshness of his philosophical outlook.

Swami Vivekananda visited England for the second time in April 1896. A pleasant surprise awaited him there. Swami Saradananda, one of his brother-disciples, who had been asked by the Swami to come to England to continue the work started during his first visit, had arrived from Calcutta and was the guest of Mr. E.T. Sturdy. This time the Swami opened regular classes on Vedantic thought; his illuminating lectures on Jnana-Yoga—the Path of Wisdom—which were as brilliant as impressive, made a direct appeal to the most intellectually gifted people of England and created a very good atmosphere for the spread of Hindu thought and culture in their purest form. He also gave several courses of lectures in public as well as to private circles.

One of the memorable events during the Swami's stay in London was his meeting with the great Orientalist, Professor Max Müller of Oxford University, at his residence, by special invitation, on May 28, 1896. To quote the Swami's own words: 'The visit was really a revelation to me. The nice little house, in its setting of a beautiful garden, the silver-headed sage, with a face calm and benign, and forehead smooth as a child's in spite of seventy winters, and every line in that face speaking of a deep-seated mine of spirituality somewhere behind....' Max Müller was anxious to know from the Swami more than what he had already gathered about Sri Ramakrishna, and told him that he would be glad to write a larger and fuller account of his Master's life and teachings. The facts, as far as available, were placed very soon by the Swami at the disposal of this venerable Professor, who set to work at once and embodied them in an instructive volume which was soon published under the title *Ramakrishna: His Life and Sayings*. The book, aided materially in giving the Swami and his mission a firmer hold on the English-speaking world.

The Swami in his previous visit had made acquaintances, which ripened into friendship, with such talented souls as Miss Henrietta Müller, Miss Margaret Nobel, Mr. E.T. Sturdy and others. Now they became his disciples and were ready to sacrifice everything for him and his cause. To this group were soon added two of his most faithful disciples, Mr. and Mrs. Sevier. Indeed the Swami held Sister Nivedita, J.J. Goodwin, and Mr. and Mrs. Sevier as the finest fruits of his work in England.

Exhausted with the strenuous exertions of his London work, the Swami accepted the invitation of three of more intimate friends for a tour and a holiday on the Continent. He spent most of the summer of 1896 in the midst of the snowy ranges of Switzerland. It was there in a village at the foot of the Alps, between Mount Blanc and the Little St. Bernard, that he first conceived the plan of founding in the silent retreat of the Himalayas a monastery where his Western and Eastern disciples might be united. And the Seviers, who were with him, never let the idea lapse; it became their life-work. While enjoying the stillness and freshness of the mountain retreat in Switzerland, there came a letter from Professor Paul Deussen, the celebrated Indologist of Germany, inviting him to visit him at Kiel. To see him the Swami shortened his stay at Switzerland. He, however, managed to visit Heidelberg, Coblenz, Cologne, and Berlin: for he wished to have a glimpse at least of Germany, and he was impressed by her material power and great learning. His reception at Kiel was as cordial and their relations as animated as might have been expected from such an ardent Vedantist as Paul Deussen.

After the continental tour the Swami again came to London, and Professor Paul Deussen joined him there. The Swami spent another two months here seeing Max Müller again, meeting Edward Carpenter, Frederick Meyers, Canon Wilberforce, and other celebrities, and delivering another series of lectures on the Vedanta, on the Hindu theory of Maya, and on the Advaita. This heavy strain seriously affected his health, and his friends suggested complete rest. But the voice of India was now calling him back. He began to feel that his part of the work in the West had been done, and it was time for him to fling himself passionately into the treadmill of action in India for the service of his motherland. For the management of his works in America in his absence, he soon sent Swami Saradananda to New York in response to the repeated requests of his disciples and students of Vedanta there; and he brought from India Swami Abhed-ananda, another of his brother-disciples, for the work in London. The Swami did all in his power to impress the newcomer with the responsibilities of his new life. Day after day he trained him so that he would be able to carry on the work alone. He was eager to leave behind a worker fitted both spiritually and intellectually to take his place, and the Swami was delighted to find in him a very able exponent of the Vedanta and a capable substitute for doing the Master's work even after his departure. Thus relieved, the mind of the Swami now pointed like the needle of a compass to India, the home of poor and sunken millions for whom he had crossed the Atlantic.

BELOVED INDIA

On December 16, 1896, the Swami with Mr. and Mrs. Sevier left London for the Continent. It was also arranged that Mr. Goodwin sailing from Southampton would meet them at Naples. The Swami rejoiced that he was free again. He said to Mr. and Mrs. Sevier, 'Now I have but one thought and that is India. I am looking forward to India!' On the eve of his departure an English friend asked, 'Swami, how do you like your motherland now after four years' experience of the luxurious, glorious, powerful West?' His significant reply was: 'India I loved before I came away. Now the very dust of India has become holy to me; it is now the holy land—the place of pilgrimage, the Tirtha.'

The party travelled to Milan via Dover, Calais, and the Mont Cenis, and had a short tour through Italy. As the train left Florence for Rome, the Swami was full of emotion, for of all cities in Europe he was most desirous to see Rome. One week was spent in this imperial city. At Rome the Swami was exceedingly delighted to witness the various places of historic importance—its magnificent seats of learning, arts, and religion. When the party left Rome, however, the Swami was not sad, for he realized that each day was bringing him nearer to the desired event—the departure for India. From Rome the next move was to Naples, where they were to embark. The ship arrived at last from Southampton, bringing Mr. Goodwin as one of its passengers, and left Naples for Colombo on December 30, 1896, with the Swami and his disciples among others, on board.

The home-coming of the Swami was a great event in the history of modern India, for a united India rose to do him honour. For about four years the Indian public had been made aware that the Swami was doing the great work of presenting and interpreting Hinduism to the Western nations with signal success. All India looked to him as to some mighty Acharya of old, born again to revivify the fading glories of the Eternal Religion and to carry her banner throughout the whole civilized world. New forces had been at play in India ever since his triumph at the Parliament of Religions. Through the study of the Swami's lectures and utterances, the eyes of the educated Indians were opened to the hidden beauties and treasures of their religion and they came more and more to see how Vedanta alone could claim the supreme position of being a universal religion.

In the early morning, on January 15, 1897,

the coast of Ceylon could be seen in the distance. It was a beautiful sight in the roseate hues of the rising sun. This was India, and the Swami was beside himself with excitement. But he was totally unaware that he was going to meet representatives of all religious sects and social bodies who had come to welcome him. One of his brother-disciples had come to Ceylon to meet him; others were on the way. In Madras and in Calcutta there was great excitement over his impending arrival. He was to find that he had become the 'man of the hour' in India.

When he arrived at Colombo, jubilant shouts arose from the seething mass of humanity covering the quays. A multitude flung itself upon him to touch his feet. A huge procession was formed with flags at its head. Religious hymns were intoned and flowers strewn before his path. Hundreds of visitors, rich and poor, brought him offerings. The cynosure of all eyes, the Swami appeared in the midst of that procession like a conqueror returning from his victory, crowned with glory—not a conqueror of earthly dominions, but a conqueror of hearts, both Eastern and Western.

In Ceylon he had to address several meetings in response to the welcome from the public. He stayed in the island for about ten days. As he crossed the sea and proceeded towards the north, everywhere he was received with most enthusiastic greetings. Triumphal processions were organized—bands played, cannons boomed, rockets shot forth as a mark of welcome, Rajas drew his carriage, and people vied with one another to show him honour and respect.

What a great difference now from the events of five years back! Then the Swami passed through these places footsore and weary —an unknown wanderer with a begging bowl in his hand. But the Swami knew that the extraordinary reception given to him was but a spontaneous expression of love of the people for the Ideal which he represented. He was now all the more convinced that religion represented the very heart of Indian national life, and all along the way he broadcasted his ideas about the regeneration of India in a series of brilliant speeches.

MESSAGE TO HIS COUNTRYMEN

Enthusiasm reached its height at Madras. The city erected for him seventeen triumphal arches, presented him with twenty-four addresses in various languages, and suspended her whole public life at his arrival. Here he gave an eloquent utterance to his message to India in a series of magnificent lectures comprising 'My Plan of Campaign', 'The Mission of Vedanta', and 'The Future of India'. 'Each nation, like each individual', he said, 'has one theme in this life, which is its centre, the principal note with which every other note mingles to form the harmony. If any nation attempts to throw off its national vitality, the direction which has become its own through the transmission of centuries, that nation dies. In India religious life forms the centre, the keynote of the whole music of national life. Social reform has to be preached in India by showing how much more spiritual a life the new system will bring, and politics has to be preached by showing how much it will improve the one thing that the nation wants— its spirituality. Therefore before flooding India with socialistic or political ideas the land should first be deluged with spiritual ideas. The first work that demands our attention is that the most wonderful truths confined in our Upanishads, in our scriptures and Puranas, must be brought out from the books, the monasteries, and the forests and scattered broadcast over the land so that these truths many run like fire all over the country, from north to south, and east to west, from the Himalayas to Cape Comorin, from the Indus to the Brahmaputra.'

'Ay, let every man and woman and child without respect of caste or birth, weakness or strength, hear and learn that behind the strong and the weak, behind the high and the low, behind everyone, there is that Infinite Soul, assuring the infinite possibility and the infinite capacity of all to become great and good. Let us proclaim to every soul: Arise, awake, and stop not till the goal is reached. Arise, awake! Awake from this hypnotism of weakness. *None* is really weak; the soul is infinite, omnipotent, and omniscient. Stand up, assert yourself, proclaim the God within you, do not deny Him.' 'It is a man-making religion that we want.... It is man-making education all round that we want. It is man-making theories that we want. And here is the test of Truth: Anything that makes you weak physically, intellectually, and spiritually, reject as poison; there is no life in it, it cannot be true. Truth is strengthening. Truth is purity, truth is all knowledge....Give up weakening mysticisms, and be strong...the greatest truths are the simplest things in the world, simple as your own existence.'

While delivering this inspiring message to his countrymen the Swami was not oblivious of his duty to emphasize the need of uplifting the sunken millions from the slough of torpor and degradation. He struck a sharp note of warning to his compatriots and gave vent to his own ideal of patriotism in the following stirring words:

'It is we who are responsible for all our degradation. Our aristocratic ancestors went on treading the common masses of our country underfoot, till they became helpless, till under this torment the poor people nearly forgot that they were human beings. They have been compelled to be merely hewers of wood and drawers of water for centuries....Feel, therefore, my would-be reformers, my would-be patriots! Do you feel? Do you feel that millions and millions of the descendants of gods and of sages have become next-door neighbours to brutes? Do you feel that millions are starving today, and millions have been starving for ages? Do you feel that ignorance has come over the land as a dark cloud? Does it make you restless?

Does it make you sleepless?...Have you forgotten all about your name, your fame, your wives, your children, your property, even your own bodies? Have you done that? That is the first step to become a patriot—the very first step....Instead of spending your energies in frothy talk, have you found any way out, any practical solution, some help instead of condemnation, some sweet words to soothe their miseries, to bring them out of this living death? Yet, that is no all. Have you got the will to surmount mountain-high obstructions? If the whole world stands against you, sword in hand, would you still dare to do what you think right?...If you have these three things, each one of you will work miracles.'

'For the next fifty years...let all other vain gods disappear...from our minds. This is the only God that is awake, our own race: everywhere His hands, everywhere His feet, everywhere His ears, He covers everything. All other gods are sleeping. What vain gods shall we go after and yet cannot worship the God that we see all round us—the Virat?...The first of all worship is the worship of the Virat—of those all around us....These are our Gods—men and animals—and the first gods we have to worship are our own countrymen....'

Bengal did not lag behind. She also vied with other provinces in giving a fitting reception to her favourite and distinguished son. Hardly had the Swami reached Calcutta when hundreds of people came to pay their personal respects to him and to hear his exposition of Vedanta. In the day-time he made his headquarters generally in the palatial building of Gopal Lal Seal at Baranagore and at night he stayed at the Math which was then at Alambazar. The City's Address of Welcome took place on 28 February 1897, at the magnificent residence of Raja Sir Radhakanta Dev Bahadur at Shobhabazar. The meeting was presided over by Raja Binoy Krishna Dev Bahadur, who introduced the Swami as the foremost national figure in the life of India. There were present Rajas and Maharajas, Sannyasins, a group of distinguished Europeans, many well-known Pandits, illustrious citizens, and hundreds of college students. The speech which the Swami gave in reply to the address of welcome has become famous as a masterpiece of oratory and of fervent patriotism.

During the Swami's stay in Calcutta he was constantly visiting one devotee of Sri Ramakrishna or another. Many distinguished people, persons of various professions and callings as well as hundreds of enthusiastic youths used to come daily to the Seal garden. The questioners were invariably charmed with his knowledge and interpretation of the Shastras, and even great masters of philosophy and university professors were amazed at his genius. But his heart was with the educated, unmarried youths, with whom he was never tired of speaking. He was consumed with the desire of infusing his own spirit into them and to train some of the more energetic and religious among them, so that they might devote their lives to the salvation of their own souls and to the good of the world. He deplored their physical weakness, denounced early marriage, admonished them for their lack of faith in themselves and in their national culture and ideals. But all this was done with such unmistakable love and kindness that they became his staunchest disciples and followers.

It goes without saying that the main interest of the Swami's stay in Calcutta centred round the Alambazar monastery. No words can describe the joy of the monks when their beloved leader was with them again. Memories of the olden days were revived, the days with the Master (Sri Ramakrishna) and the innumerable experiences of the wandering life of everyone were recalled, and the Swami entertained his Gurubhais (brother-disciples) and the devotees of the Master with hundreds of tales and episodes of his life and work in the distant West.

Of the Swami's numerous achievements one of the greatest was the conversion of his Gurubhais from the individualistic to the universal idea of religious life in which public spirit and service to fellow-men occupied a prominent place. Up to this time the ideal of the monks of the Math was to strive for personal Mukti (liberation) and realization of the Supreme Atman by severe penance and meditation, remaining as much as possible aloof from the world, its cares and sorrows, in consonance with the old conception of monastic life. But with the appearance of the Swami among them a new order of things was inaugurated. He railed at them for their lack of faith in themselves and in the great mission of the Master, for their failure to organize themselves into an active body, and for their neglect in preaching the gospel of liberation to others. The age demanded, he said, that they should carry the new light unto others, that they themselves should show by their example how to serve the poor, the helpless, and the diseased, seeing God in them, and that they should inspire others to do the same. The mission of his life, he declared, was to create a new order of Sannyasins in India who would dedicate their lives to help and serve others. Thus the Swami interpreted his Master's message in a new light, showing them that their supreme duty lay in the carrying on of the Master's mission, the bringing about of a religious rejuvenation by raising the condition of the masses through loving service, and spreading the life-giving ideas of the Master over the entire world. Even while in the West he had conveyed to his Gurubhais this message again and again through his inspiring letters. Now, his personal presence and passionate appeals as also his brilliant exposition of his Master's mission completely bore down all opposition and he electrified their imagination with the synthetic ideal which combined in it a life of renunciation and service —a course of strict moral discipline, contemplation, and study as also of self-dedication at the altar of humanity for the attainment of the highest goal of human existence.

Out of their profound faith in their leader, his brother-disciples bowed their heads in acquiescence, knowing his voice to be the voice of their Master; all girded up their loins to do anything and to go anywhere, for the good of their fellow-beings at the bidding of the Swami. Swami Ramakrishnananda, who had never left the precincts of the Math for twelve years, went to Madras at the behest of Swami Vivekananda to open a centre there to propagate the teachings of the Vedanta in Southern India. Swamis Saradananda and Abhedananda had already gone to the West at the call of the Swami to help him in the work there. And full of the same spirit, Swami Akhandananda went to the district of Murshidabad to start famine relief work for the people dying from starvation in the villages. The other Gurubhais of the Swami were also ready to take up, as occasion demanded, any work of religious and philanthropic utility launched by him, or to further his ideas and plans of work in India and abroad. A brilliant group of young men inspired by the Swami's life and teachings soon joined the Order and now gallantly stood by his side to sacrifice their lives for others, to provide the ignorant and the depressed masses with the ways and means for the struggle for existence and make them stand on their own feet, to preach the highest message of the scriptures to one and all. Gradually there came into existence the various monastic centres, Homes of Service, and the relief centres in times of plague, famine, and flood, under the charge and with the co-operation of his Gurubhais and his disciples.

The Swami had long thought of bringing about a co-operative effort among the monastic and the lay disciples of Sri Ramakrishna, and of organizing in a systematic way the activities, both spiritual and philanthropic, of his Guru-bhais. In response to the Swami's intimation of his desire to hold a meeting for the purpose of founding an association, a representative gather-ing of all the monastic and lay disciples of Sri Ramakrishna took place at the house of a devotee—Balaram Bose—in the afternoon of 1 May 1897. With the unanimous consent of the assembled devotees an organization was formed under the name of the Ramakrishna Mission Association.

The duty of the Mission would be to conduct in the right spirit the activities of the movement inaugurated by Sri Ramakrishna for the establishment of fellowship among the fol-lowers of different religions, knowing them all to be so many forms only of one underlying Eternal Religion. Its methods of action would be (1) to train men so as to make them competent to teach such knowledge or sciences as are conducive to the material and spiritual welfare

7

of the masses; (2) to promote and encourage arts and industries; (3) to introduce and spread among the people in general Vedantic and other religious ideas in the way in which they were elucidated in the life of Sri Ramakrishna. It was further resolved that the activities of this Mission should be directed to the establishment of Maths and Ashramas in different parts of India for the training of Sannyasins and such of the householders as may be willing to devote their lives to educate others. Its work in the foreign department should be to send trained members of the Order to countries outside India to start centres there for the preaching of Vedanta in order to bring about a close relation and better understanding between India and foreign countries.[3]

A practical Vedantist, Swami Vivekananda wanted one and all to translate the Upanishadic doctrines into action in everyday life. The Swami himself practised the ideal in his own life; he flung himself whole-heartedly into the whirlpool of activity and thus inspired others to follow in his footsteps and render service to the

3. Afterwards, when the Belur Math was established, this Association ceased to function as an independent organization. But out of this nucleus has gown the present Ramakrishna Mission, which became a registered body in 1909.

suffering humanity even under the most trying circumstances.

From May 1897 to January 1898, he went like a whirlwind through the historic cities of Northern India, sowing the seed with his characteristic boldness and zeal. Whether at Almora, Kashmir, and the Punjab, or at Khetri, Alwar, Ajmer, and other principal states of Rajputana —in every place the Swami was the recipient of spontaneous homage of his countrymen from the highest to the lowest. He mixed and talked as freely and intimately with the Rajas and Maharajas as with other sections of the Indian people—always placing before them the vital needs of their motherland.

He was never tired of showing to his countrymen the value and significance of the culture they had inherited from their ancestors—a culture in comparison with which any other civilization, past or present, paled into insignificance—till their hearts throbbed at the very name of India. He clearly pointed out that Indian nationalism was to be based on the greatness of the past though various new ideas also had to be assimilated in the process of growth. If we have to be true to the genius of the race, if we have to appeal to the soul of the nation, we have to drink deep of the fountain of the past and then proceed to build the future. This heritage from the past, he pointed out, was essentially a religious heritage. The fundamental problem in India, therefore, was to organize the whole country round the spiritual ideal. By religion he meant the eternal life-giving principles as taught by the Shrutis and not the mass of superstitions and local customs, which are mere accretions requiring a weeding out with a strong hand. Above all, he showed that the nation depended upon the character and qualities of its individual members. On the strength of the individuals lay the strength of the whole nation. So each individual, he urged, if he desired the good of the country as a whole, should try, whatever might be his walk of life, to build character and acquire such virtues as courage, strength, and self-respect, and practice the national ideals of renunciation and service.

IN THE COMPANY OF WESTERN
AND EASTERN DISCIPLES

Having finished his lecture tour Swami Vivekananda returned to Calcutta about the middle of January 1898. The Math was transferred in February from Alambazar to Nilambar Mukherjee's garden-house on the western bank of the Ganga in the village of Belur. For some time the Swami devoted himself to certain important aspects of his Mission—notably the training of his own disciples, both Eastern and Western, so as to enable them to carry into practice his plans for the regeneration of his motherland. His Western disciples had come to India at his call: Miss Margaret Noble at the end of January, to found in conjunction with Miss Henrietta F. Müller model institutions for the education of Indian women; Mrs. Ole Bull and Miss Josephine MacLeod in February. In March, Margaret Noble took the vow of Brahmacharya and the name of Nivedita, the Consecrated One. Vivekananda introduced her in warm terms to the Calcutta public as a gift of England to India.

The training of these Western disciples was of momentous concern to the Swami as a spiritual teacher. Among the Western disciples he particularly chose Nivedita in whom he had great hope and trust; and as such, his illuminating discourses were mainly directed to her. The Swami was anxious that his Western disciples should make an impartial study of Indian problems. They were not only to see the glories, but also to have special and clear understanding of the problems of the land and to bring the ideals and methods of Western scientific culture to bear upon the task of finding a solution.

The Swami then set out on a journey through India with a select group of his disciples. After a stay at Almora, were the Seviers were already established, and then after a journey to Kashmir up the river Jhelum through the Vale of Srinagar, the Swami undertook, at the end of July 1898, the great pilgrimage to the cave of Amarnath in the glacial gorge of the Western Himalayas. Only Sister Nivedita was permitted to accompany him to that holy place. On August 2, the day of the annual festival, they arrived at the sacred cave where there was the famous ice-Shiva. Behind the other pilgrims, Swami Vivekananda, trembling with emotion, entered the sanctuary in an almost semi-conscious condition. A great mystical experience came to him. So saturated became his personality with the Presence of the

Lord that for days afterwards he could speak of nothing but Shiva—the Eternal One, the Great Monk, rapt in meditation, aloof from all worldliness.

Following the pilgrimage to Amarnath the Swami's devotion concentrated itself on the Mother, and he was soon blessed with a wonderful vision of Kali the Divine Mother. While his vision was most intense he wrote 'Kali the Mother'—a poem, where he is seen at his best. After this experience he retired alone abruptly on September 30 to the Coloured Springs of Kshir Bhavani where he practised severe austerities. He was found completely transfigured when he returned to his disciples after a few days. All thought of leader, worker, or teacher was gone. He was now only the Monk—in all nakedness of pure Sannyasa. So, he feelingly said to them, 'It is all "Mother" now! All my patriotism is gone. Everything is gone. Now it is only "Mother, Mother"!' The party then came back to Lahore. The Swami's health was so much undermined that he had to be brought back to Bengal by Swami Sadananda, who had hurried down from Almora after learning of the Swami's poor health.

They arrived at Belur, where the new monastery was under construction, in the month of October. The Swami, in spite of his failing health, resumed his old life with the monks and performed the consecrating ceremony of the monastery on December 9. From January 2, 1899, this place, now known as Belur Math, became the permanent headquarters of the monks of the Ramakrishna Order. Gathering together his disciples, the Swami began from now to impress on them the duties and responsibilities of their monastic life. Hours were spent in religious conversation; scriptures were read and commented upon; and strict regulations and monastic discipline were instituted along with spiritual and intellectual work for certain hours of the day. Addressing the disciples, the Swami would point out, 'The history of the world is the history of a few men who had faith in themselves. That faith calls out the divinity within. You fail only when you do not strive sufficiently to manifest infinite power. As soon as a man loses faith in himself, death comes. Believe first in yourself, and then in God. A handful of strong men will move the world. It is the salvation of others that you must seek; and even if you have to go to hell in working for others, that is worth more than to gain heaven by seeking your own salvation.'

In spite of illness, the Swami continued

with the organization of the Ramakrishna Mission with Swami Saradananda who had been called back from America for this work. He soon built up a strong band of 'the sappers and miners in the army of religion' for the reconstruction of Indian life, as also for the diffusion of Vedantic ideas throughout the length and breadth of the world. Very soon, his dream of starting a monastery in a cool, secluded region of the Himalayas, where the East and the West could meet on an equal footing of love and unity, exchange the highest ideals of each, and practise the Advaita philosophy, was also realized. Mr. and Mrs. Sevier with the help of Swami Swarupananda, founded the Advaita Ashrama in March 1899, under the guidance of Swami Vivekananda at Mayavati from where one can command a magnificent view of the charming ranges of perpetual snow. Other service institutions also sprang into existence under his directions in different parts of India, and the Swami had the satisfaction of seeing his lofty ideal rooted deep in the soil of his birth.

SECOND VISIT TO THE WEST

The Swami announced his intention of going to the West in order to see the work he had founded as well as to give fresh impetus to them. He was urged also by his friends and physicians to do so at once as his health was very poor. This time he took with him Sister Nivedita and a brother monk, Swami Turiyananda, and boarded the steamer on June 20, 1899. In regard to taking Swami Turiyananda to America, the Swami said, 'They have seen the Kshatriya power—now I want to show them the Brahmin!' He meant that in himself the West had seen the combative spirit and energy in the defence of the Eternal Religion, Sanatana Dharma; and now the time had come when the people should have before them the example of a man of meditation in his Gurubhai, born and bred in the best traditions and rigorous discipline of Brahminhood. After having broken his journey in London, he went to the United States and stayed for almost a year. There he found Abhedananda actively engaged in the Vedantic work. Turiyananda settled down at Mont Clair near New York, and he himself went to California, where he founded the Vedanta Society at San Francisco. Besides, he received the gift of a property of one hundred and sixty acres of forest land in the district of Santa Clara, where an Ashrama was established by Swami Turiyananda to train a select band of students in the monastic life. Thus the work prospered and the ideas spread.

But though the Swami was full of merriment even while busy consolidating his work in America, there was always in him the undertone of serious states of mind. Throughout his Western experience this time one notices in him a deep yearning for the Absolute. In one of his letters he definitely says, '...pray for me...that my works may stop for ever, and my whole soul be absorbed in the Mother....The battles are lost and won. I have bundled my things, and am waiting for the Great Deliverer....I am only the boy who used to listen with rapt wonderment to the wonderful words of Ramakrishna under the banyan of Dakshineswar. That is my true nature; works and activities, doing good and so forth are all superimpositions. Now, I again hear his voice; the same old voice thrilling my soul. Bonds are breaking, love dying, work becoming tasteless; the glamour is off life. Now only the voice of the Master calling..."Let the dead bury the dead, follow thou Me." "I come, my Beloved Lord, I come"...Nirvana is before me. I feel it at times, the same infinite ocean of peace, without a ripple, a breath.'

Towards the end of July 1900, the Swami started for Paris, where he had been invited to the Congress of the History of Religions. He stayed in Paris for about three months and left for Egypt *via* Vienna, Constantinople, and Athens. The meditative habit, which had revealed itself ever since his second visit to the West in intense forms, now reached a veritable climax. In Paris, oftentimes his mind had been far aloof from his environment; and here in Egypt it seemed as if he were turning the last pages in the Book of Experience. He seemed world-weary.

Suddenly he felt a strong desire to return to India. There in the far-off Himalayan Ashrama, Mr. Sevier, his great friend and disciple, had given up his body—a martyr to his cause. The Swami had, as it were, a presentiment of this. He became restless to return to India. So without waiting a single day he took the first steamer and came back alone to his motherland at the beginning of December 1900. The joy of his brother-monks knew no bounds when they unexpectedly found their leader present in their midst.

About his impression of this visit to the

West the Swami said that during his first journey he had been caught by the power, the organization, and the apparent democracy of America and Europe. But now he had discovered the spirit of lucre, of greed, of Mammon, with its enormous combinations and ferocious struggle for supremacy. Material brilliance no longer deceived him. He saw the hidden tragedy, the weariness under the forced expenditure of energy—the deep sorrow under the frivolous mask. 'Social life in the West,' he said to Nivedita, 'is like a peal of laughter: but underneath it is a wail. It ends in a sob. The fun and frivolity are all on the surface; really it is full of tragic intensity....Here (in India) it is sad and gloomy on the surface, but underneath are carelessness and merriment.'

PARTING GLIMPSES

Before taking up the work that awaited him on his return to India, the Swami's first object was to visit Mrs. Sevier at the Advaita Ashrama, in Mayavati. On his arrival at the Belur Math, he had the confirmation of his premonition of the passing away of his beloved disciple, Mr. Sevier, which had occurred on October 28, 1900. Without stopping to rest at Belur, he telegraphed to Mayavati that he was coming to the Ashrama. He arrived on January 3, 1901, and despite the mingled joy and emotion he felt at meeting Mrs. Sevier again, in seeing the work finished, and in contemplating the beauty of the Ashrama perched on the mountain-slope he could stay there only for a fortnight; asthma suffocated him. The Swami had to come back to the Belur Math on January 24. Apart from a last pilgrimage that he made with his mother to the holy places of Eastern Bengal and Assam, to Dacca and Shillong, which left him exhausted, he left Belur only for a short stay at Varanasi at the beginning of 1902. The great journey of his life was soon to end.

After his return from the tour in East Bengal and Assam, which was the last public tour undertaken by the Swami, his health was much worse. The monks were greatly concerned. They now urged him to have complete rest; they begged him to give up all thought of appearing before the public until he should be perfectly well. But as was his wont, he gave frequent interviews to all who flocked to the Belur Math in these days from all parts of India to receive his blessings and instructions.

At the monastery he lived a simple life, free from the monotony of society and its tiresome conventionalities. He was a 'Sannyasin free'. He would freely walk about barefooted or with plain slippers on and sometimes with a staff in hand—full of mirth like a boy. Here he was free of the necessity to dress according to the dictates of society. With a *kaupin* or a piece of Gerua (ochre) cloth on, he could live in a world of his own in monastic silence and seclusion. At times he would be found taking interest in the garden or experimenting in cooking or finding delight in the company of his pet animals— 'Bagha' the dog, 'Hansi' the she-goat, 'Matru' the kid, an antelope, a stork, cows, and so on. At this time who could recognize in him the world-renowned Swami Vivekananda! At other times he would instruct or help the members of the Math in their difficulties, always manifesting the greatest tenderness. Almost daily until his passing, he held Vedantic classes to teach the novices the methods of meditation, inspired the workers with a spirit of virile confidence in themselves, paid strict attention to discipline and cleanliness, drew up a weekly timetable and kept a watchful eye over the regularity of all the daily activities. No negligence escaped the vigilance of the Swami. He always maintained an atmosphere of serene peace and holiness. He was the irresistible magnet and the inmates of the Ashrama were as so many iron filings drawn towards him, often without understanding why, but always loving him. Every word of this great teacher was instinct with life and vigour and acted with telling effect on all who listened.

Once when he saw some monks and Brahmacharins going for worship to the temple, he said to them, 'Where shall you go to seek Brahman? He is immanent in all beings. *Here*, *here* is the visible Brahman! Shame on those who, neglecting the visible Brahman, set their minds on other things. *Here* is the Brahman before you as tangible as a fruit in one's hand!' So forceful was his utterance that everyone felt an ineffable peace and remained for nearly a quarter of an hour rooted to the spot. The scene was unforgettable. Everyone in the monastery was struck with amazement at the wonderful power of the beloved Leader who with but one word could raise the minds of all to the heights of Supreme Insight.

About the latter part of the year 1901, a number of *Santal* labourers used to work in the Math grounds. One day he served a beautiful feast for them at which he said, 'You are Narayanas; today I have entertained Narayana Himself.' Then turning towards his disciples, he said to them, 'See how simple-hearted these poor illiterate people are. Will you be able to relieve their miseries to some extent at least? Otherwise, of what use is our wearing the Gerua (the ochre robe of the Sannyasin)?...How can we have the heart to put a morsel into our mouths when our countrymen have not enough wherewith to feed or clothe themselves?...Let us throw away all pride of learning and study of the Shastras and all Sadhanas for the attainment of personal Mukti—and going from village to village devote our lives to the service of the poor, and by convincing the rich men about their duties to the masses, through the force of our character and spirituality and austere living, get money and the means wherewith to serve the poor and the distressed. Alas! Nobody in

8

our country thinks for the low, the poor, and the miserable! Those that are the backbone of the nation, whose labour produces food, those whose one day's strike from work raises a cry of general distress in the city—where is the man in our country who sympathizes with them, who shares in their joys and sorrows?...Unless they are elevated, the great Mother (India) will never awake!...What I see clear as daylight is that the same Brahman, the same Shakti is in them as in me! Only there is a difference in the degree of manifestation—that is all. In the whole history of the world have you ever seen a country rise unless there was a uniform circulation of the national blood all over its body? Know this for certain, that no great work can be done by that body, one limb of which is paralysed....After so much Tapasya (asceticism) I have known that the highest truth is this: He is present in every being! These are all the manifold forms of Him. There is no other God to seek for! He alone is worshipping God who serves all beings!'

The days glided by in the Math as if they were hours. Whatever the mood in which the Swami might be, for his Gurubhais and disciples his presence was in itself a constant source of joy and inspiration. Whether he was

impatient, whether he reprimanded, whether he
was the teacher or the meditating sage, whether
he was full of mirth or grave—to his Gurubhais
he was always the beloved 'Naren', and to his
disciples the blessed and incomparable Guru.
The joy of the Swami was great when meditation and austerities were in full swing in the
Math. Whenever his health permitted, he joined
in the morning meditation in the chapel. His
presence in the meditation room invariably lent
an added power and intensity to the meditations of those who sat with him.

In spite of his physical ailment, the Swami
was eager till the end to receive friends and
visitors and instruct his disciples. Everything
must be sacrificed, even the body itself. Sometimes hearing of the plight of earnest seekers
who were refused admission to his presence by
the monks, he would be so deeply moved with
pity that he would say, 'Look here! Did not the
Master preach unto the very end? And shall I
not do the same? I do not care a straw if the
body goes! You cannot imagine how happy I
am when I find earnest seekers after truth to
talk to. In the work of waking up the Atman in
my fellow-men I shall gladly die again and
again!' But on some other occasions, in the
midst of his talks his face would assume a

dreamy far-away look and then all would leave him, knowing that he wished to be left alone with his thoughts.

THE PASSING

The last two months which the Swami
passed on earth were full of events fore-
shadowing the approaching end, though at
times these events passed by unsuspected by
those around him. As days passed the Swami
felt more and more the necessity of with-
drawing himself from the task of directing the
affairs of the Math. 'How often,' he said, 'does
a man ruin his disciples by remaining always
with them? When men are once trained, it is
essential that their leader leaves them, for
without his absence they cannot develop themselves!' Work and all other bonds were drop-
ping off; more than ever did he withdraw himself from all outer concerns. Meditation became
his one great occupation. His Gurubhais and
disciples were alarmed at seeing him retire into
such an atmosphere of austerity and meditation.
The prophecy of Sri Ramakrishna that Naren
would merge in Nirvikalpa Samadhi at the end
of his works constantly haunted their memory.

It seemed he was looking forward to a
certain day on which to throw off the bondage
of the body. It was Friday, the fourth of July
1902. On that day he went to the chapel in the
morning, and after closing the windows and

bolting the doors, spent three hours in meditation. Then he broke forth in a touching song of the Divine Mother. The monks below were charmed to hear the sweet strains of it coming from the shrine-room.

Descending the stairs of the shrine, he paced up and down in the courtyard of the monastery, his mind withdrawn. He was heard muttering to himself: 'If there were another Vivekananda, he would have understood what Vivekananda has done! And yet, how many Vivekanandas shall be born in time!' The Gurubhai who, unnoticed, heard these words was startled, for never did the Swami speak in this manner.

At noon he took his food along with all in the refectory—contrary to his practice during these days. After the meal he took a Sanskrit class with his disciples for about three hours. Then in the afternoon he took a walk with one of his Gurubhais and expressed his particular desire to establish a Vedic College in the Math. In the evening, as the service bell in the shrine rang, he went to his room and remained absorbed in meditation for nearly an hour. Then he laid himself down on his bed. He had his rosary still in his hand. About an hour later, he changed sides and took a deep breath. Another long deep breath like the preceding one, and then all was calm and still. The tired child slept in the lap of the Mother, whence there was no awakening to this world of Maya.

The Swami was thirty-nine years and a few months, thus fulfilling a prophecy which was frequently on his lips, 'I shall never live to see forty.' But with the passing of days, as one observes how the number of his disciples, devotees, and admirers in the two hemispheres is rapidly increasing, how he is silently influencing thousands of lives all over the world, how his fiery message is supplying direct and indirect inspiration to hundreds of movements in his own motherland and throughout the world for the uplift of which he thought so much and worked so hard—one remembers the words he spoke long before his death: 'It may be that I shall find it good to get outside my body—to cast it off like a worn-out garment. But I shall not cease to work! I shall inspire men everywhere, until the world shall know that it is one with God!'

SOME UTTERANCES

Ye divinities on earth—sinners! It is a sin to call a man so; it is a standing libel on human nature. Come up, O lions, and shake off the delusion that you are sheep; you are souls immortal, spirits free, blest and eternal; ye are not matter, ye are not bodies; matter is your servant, not you the servant of matter.

★ ★ ★

If you have faith in the three hundred and thirty millions of your mythological gods, and in all gods which foreigners have introduced into your midst, and still have no faith in yourselves, there is no salvation for you. Have faith in yourselves and stand up on that faith.

★ ★ ★

The history of the world is the history of a few men who had faith in themselves. That faith calls out the Divinity within. You can do anything. You fail only when you do not strive sufficiently to manifest infinite power. As soon as a man or a nation loses faith in himself or itself, death comes.

Believe first in yourself, and then in God.

* * *

He is an atheist who does not believe in himself. The old religions said that he was an atheist who did not believe in God; the new religion says that he is the atheist who does not believe in himself.

* * *

The Voice of Asia has been the voice of religion. The Voice of Europe is the voice of politics.

* * *

India is immortal, if she persists in her search for God.

* * *

I do not mean to say that political or social improvements are not necessary, but what I mean is this, and I want you to bear it in mind, that they are secondary here, and that religion is primary.

* * *

None can resist her (India) any more; never is

she going to sleep any more; no outward powers can hold her back any more; for the infinite giant is rising to her feet.

★ ★ ★

If you seek your own salvation, you will go to hell. It is the salvation of others that you must seek; and even if you have to go to hell in working for others, that is worth more than to gain heaven by seeking your own salvation.

★ ★ ★

So long as the millions die in hunger and ignorance, I hold every man a traitor who, having been educated at their expense, pays not the least heed to them!

★ ★ ★

So long as even a single dog in my country is without food, my whole religion will be to feed it.

★ ★ ★

Where should you go to seek for God? Are not all the poor, the miserable, the weak, gods?

Why not worship them first? Why go to dig a well on the shores of the Ganga? Let these people be your God—think of them, work for them, pray for them incessantly—the Lord will show you the way.

★   ★   ★

Religion deals with the truths of the metaphysical world, just as chemistry and the other natural sciences deal with the truths of the physical world.

★   ★   ★

Take religion from human society and what will remain? Nothing but a forest of brutes. Sense happiness is not the goal of humanity; wisdom (Jnana) is the goal of all life.

★   ★   ★

The ultimate goal of all mankind, the aim and end of all religions, is but one—reunion with God, or, what amounts to the same, with the divinity which is every man's true nature.

★   ★   ★

Can religion really accomplish anything? It can. It brings to man eternal life. It has made man what he is and will make of this human animal, a God. That is what religion can do. The ideal of all religions, all sects, is the same—the attaining of liberty, the cessation of misery.

★ ★ ★

I claim that no destruction of religion is necessary to improve the Hindu society, and that this state of society exists not on account of religion, but because religion has not been applied to society as it should have been.

★ ★ ★

Let there be but a dozen lion-souls in each country, lions who have broken their own bounds, who have touched the Infinite, whose whole soul is gone to Brahman, who care neither for wealth, nor power, nor fame, and these will be enough to shake the world.

★ ★ ★

My ideal indeed can be put into a few words, and that is: to preach unto mankind their divinity, and how to make it manifest in every movement of life.

* * *

Those who give themselves up to the Lord do more for the world than all the so-called workers.

* * *

What we need today is to know that there is a God, and that we can see and feel Him here and now.

* * *

Not a drop will be in the ocean, not a twig in the deepest forest, not a crumb in the house of the god of wealth, if the Lord is not merciful. Streams will be in the desert and the beggar will have plenty if He wills it. He seeth the sparrow's fall. Are these but words or literal, actual life?

* * *

This life is short, the vanities of the world are transient, but they alone live who live for others, the rest are more dead than alive.

* * *

These prophets were not unique; they were men as you or I. They were great Yogis. They had gained this superconsciousness, and you and I can get the same. The very fact that one man ever reached that state, proves that it is possible for every man to do so. Not only is it possible, but every man must, eventually, get to that state, and that is religion.

★ ★ ★

The only true duty is to be unattached and to work as free beings, to give up all work unto God. All duties are His.

★ ★ ★

No work is secular. All work is adoration and worship.

★ ★ ★

As I grow older I find that I look more and more for greatness in *little* things. Anyone will be great in a great position. Even the coward will grow brave in the glare of the footlights. The world looks on! More and more the true greatness seems to me that of the worm doing its duty silently, steadily from moment to moment and hour to hour.

★　★　★

We want everything but God, because our ordinary desires are fulfilled by the external world. So long as our needs are confined within the limits of the physical universe, we do not feel any need for God; it is only when we have had hard blows in our lives and are disappointed with everything here that we feel the need for something higher; then we seek God.

★　★　★

Life is the unfoldment and development of a being under circumstances tending to press it down.

★　★　★

There must be no fear. No begging, but demanding—*demanding* the Highest. The true devotees of the Mother are as hard as adamant and as fearless as lions. They are not the least upset if the whole universe suddenly crumbles into dust at their feet! *Make* Her listen to you. None of that *cringing* to Mother! Remember, She is all-powerful. She can make heroes even out of *stones*!

*   *   *

Each soul is potentially divine. The goal is to manifest this divinity within by controlling nature, external and internal. Do this either by work, or worship, or psychic control, or philosophy—by one or more or all of these—and be free. This is the whole of religion. Doctrines or dogmas or rituals or books or temples or forms are but secondary details.

*   *   *

Each soul is a star, and all stars are set in that infinite azure, that eternal sky, the Lord. There is the root, the reality, the real individuality of each and all. Religion began with the search after some of these stars that had passed beyond our horizon, and ended in finding them all in God, and ourselves in the same place.